BASEBALL PIONEERS

To Rocky

Shirley Burkovich

Maybelle Blair

BASEBALL PIONEERS

**True stories of guts and glory
as told by the pioneering
men and women of the game**

Edited by KELLY HOLTZCLAW
and JON LEONOUDAKIS

Foreword by ARNOLD HANO

EVZONE MEDIA + EXPERIENTIAL   **Facetious Publishing**

The Sweet Spot books are available at discounts for bulk
quantities for sales and promotional use. For more details
contact Sales Manager at publishingsales@thesweetspot.tv

ISBN 978-0-9989193-1-7

Editors: Kelly Holtzclaw and Jon Leonoudakis
Foreword: Arnold Hano
Interior Book Design: Kelly Holtzclaw
Cover Design: Brian Goings and Brian Kruse

CONTENTS

INTRODUCTION

*"I don't even like baseball, but I love these human stories
you tell."*
—*A fan of "The Sweet Spot" streaming TV series*

Once upon a time, a man named Lawrence Ritter made a personal
journey to gather the stories and recollections of baseball players
who took the field from 1898-1947.

Those recordings rendered untold stories, insight, and an eye-
witness account of the national pastime as it grew to become the
top sport in America. From those interviews, Ritter would craft
one of baseball's most iconic books, *The Glory of Their Times*. This
book was the chief inspiration behind the creation of a new multimedia project we've embarked upon, *The Sweet Spot: A Treasury
of Baseball Stories*.

Since narrative has always been at the heart of baseball, we
wanted to create a project that would share inside, untold stories, but
with a twist: our goal was to focus on the human side of the game.
We wanted to explore stories from those who weave the tapestry
of baseball in America: coaches, players, fans, writers, umpires,
clubhouse managers, and the myriad crewmembers that support

the game. It was also important that we not only include war stories, but a perspective on social and cultural issues in baseball, like race, gender, and the impact of art and literature on the game.

The Sweet Spot has always been intended as a multimedia project. While our streaming TV documentary series on Amazon, ROKU, and Vimeo on Demand is our calling card, these books allow us to compile edited transcripts of our interviews and share them with sports fans, historians, and culture vultures.

We hope these stories will help fill in the blanks for parts of baseball history and add to the historical narrative of what Babe Ruth called, "the greatest game."

This book was put together by two college friends who reunited some thirty years after graduating from Loyola Marymount University's film school in Los Angeles. Kelly Holtzclaw is a new media publisher and social media strategist, as well as a maker of fine wines. Jon Leonoudakis is an award-winning producer, filmmaker, and baseball documentarian with six films in the permanent collection of the National Baseball Hall of Fame.

There's something very different about this baseball book. Of the six individuals featured, four are women. We're advocates of women in baseball and feel they have been on the short end of the stick since 1909 when Albert G. Spalding proclaimed, "Base Ball is too strenuous for womankind." Even with the deck stacked against them, many women have impacted the landscape of the game, and we're pleased to give some of them their due.

The journey to collect these stories has been as remarkable as the individuals who opened their homes and hearts to us. Our interviews are recorded on video and audio, and once we start rolling, we usually talk for about an hour. There were some exceptions: umpire Perry Barber gave us twenty minutes of her time before donning a mask and calling a game. Jim "Mudcat" Grant sat with us in his home and talked for two and a half hours! We could've easily spent a week talking with Mudcat, who is not only a great storyteller, he's an American treasure.

This book marks the end of a remarkable first year for *The Sweet Spot*, where a very small group of people put together three seasons of shows for our documentary series and this book. *Baseball Pioneers* is just the first volume of a series of books from our initial collection of over thirty interviews. We hope you'll make room on your bookshelves for future volumes, which will feature stories from baseball card photographers, artists, actors, scorekeepers, super-fans, and much, much more.

You can take a deeper dive into our celebration of baseball by visiting our website at www.thesweetspot.tv. You'll find our collection of custom baseball cards, "Heroes of the Sweet Spot" (some of which are featured in every chapter of this book) available for purchase along with our snazzy, eye-popping t-shirts.

It's time to grab a cold one and a hot dog because somewhere in the distance, two of the most important words in the English language are about to be uttered: "Play ball!"

—*Jon Leonoudakis*

FOREWORD

The far-too-brief commissioner of baseball, Bart Giamatti, once said, "Baseball will break your heart." And he added a second sentence, which I do not understand: "Baseball is intended to break your heart." Something must have happened because it broke his heart and he was dead long before his time.

As a long-time Giants fan, New York Giants and now San Francisco Giants, I know what it is to suffer a broken heart. I just look at the standings every day. My friend Jon Leonoudakis has produced a series of oral histories that will in most cases break your heart and also elevate your spirit. For instance, there's Justine Siegal, who told a male friend she intended to be a baseball coach. He scoffed. "They won't listen to you," he said, dismissing her. She took those words to heart and went about studying baseball, coaches talking to baseball people, doing everything that she had to do to satisfy herself. When she was ready, she presented herself, and after a few sentences, it was clear she knew what she was talking about, and they listened to her. She became a baseball coach.

Then you will learn more about the inside of baseball from pitcher Maybelle Blair and utility player Shirley Burkovich of the All-American Girls Professional Baseball League. When they told Jon that they played the game before they had uniforms, he asked a question that they seemed to bristle with astonishment: "you played in skirts?!"

They played in their skirts. They exemplify in this book the secret mantra of success. They would become part of the game. And when they finished a game, they compared strawberries. Now to some of you, a strawberry is a piece of fruit. But to those of us who played before we had uniforms, the strawberry was the trademark of the game. It was the size usually of a half-dollar, maybe bigger. A red bruise as red as a strawberry, from which you often picked out pieces of dirt.

I don't know why they call it sandlot ball. In the Bronx when my brother and I played before we had uniforms, it was a dirt lot, not a sandlot. And we compared strawberries at the end of any session. We did this quietly because had my mother heard us, she would have said, "You've got bruises? That's the end of it, no more baseball." I don't know what she would have expected us to play instead. Football? That is the true essence of Jon's book. You become part of the game and if you don't, go out looking for a clerical job.

One of my favorites here is the umpire, Perry Barber. Perry has been umpiring since 1981. She has learned to umpire and to achieve umpire success. It is not just knowing the difference between safe and out, fair or foul, strike or ball. It's how you do it. She talks about the flow of the game. Her prose is as good as anything that came out of Haywood Broun's mouth or even mine. It's too lovely for me to tell you here, read it for yourself.

I think I know what some of this is about. When I was 10 or 11, I took my friend, Marion Rose, to the Polo Grounds bleachers in 1933. When we went up the ramp to the wooden planks, she looked around and grabbed my arm. "No women," she said. Then we looked at each other, nodded and went to our seats. Marion knew how to become part of the game. In a middle inning, Travis Jackson, the Giant shortstop, lofted a fly ball along the left field foul line that grazed the upper deck seats in left field and fell on the grass for a home run. A fan chortled, "Chinese home run, Travis!"

Marion, said, "What's that mean?" I explained, "A Chinese home run is not a real blast but something that barely squeezes by." She said, "has anybody else hit one today?" I said, "No." She stood up, clapped her hands and said, "Atta baby Travis," and sat down. She'd become a true bleacherite.

There are some ugly moments in this book. We learn through Jim "Mudcat" Grant that black pitchers were never going to be allowed to be twenty-game winners. I don't know how they intended to do that, but I think there were lots of different ways. You can miss a turn or two. You can be placed on whatever thing they had before the disabled list. But twenty games makes the difference between good and great. Carl Hubbell. Bob "Lefty" Grove. Dizzy Dean. Others of that small ilk. Blacks are not welcome to join. Grant even went so far to suggest that a catcher, white, would whisper to a batter, white, what pitch was coming. Fastball. Curveball. Thrown by a pitcher, black.

Now, I told this to a friend of mine who played baseball with Tom Seaver at USC. He said, "it can't be, the ump would have overheard." So there you are. Maybe it was said in such a hushed tone, or maybe the umpire didn't give a damn.

Baseball is not always easy. Even Jackie Robinson found it hard to swallow. He didn't pull any punches. He let his bitterness be known. Ron Rapoport tells you all about it, here.

So that's it. This is baseball with an edge. It will, if you are perceptible, break your heart. But perhaps, the commissioner was right. That is baseball's intention, but Jon is able to elevate it. And I for one, ended up feeling high.

—*Arnold Hano*
September 2017

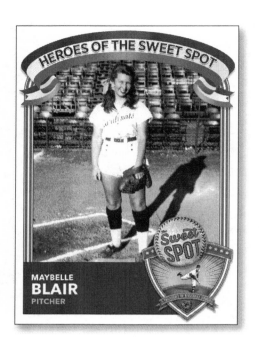

HEROES OF THE SWEET SPOT

MAYBELLE
BLAIR
PITCHER

HEROES OF THE SWEET SPOT

SHIRLEY
BURKOVICH
INFIELD-OUTFIELD

MAYBELLE BLAIR & SHIRLEY BURKOVICH

We are the members of the All-American League.
We come from cities near and far.
We've got Canadians, Irishmen, and Swedes,
We're all for one, were one for all
We're All-Americans!

—Verse from the official song of the All-American Girls Profes-
sional Baseball League, co-written by Lavonne "Pepper" Paire
Davis and Nalda "Bird" Phillips

MAYBELLE BLAIR–PITCHER

This colorful right-handed pitcher from Inglewood, California took the hill for the Peoria Red Wings of the All-American Girls Professional Baseball League. She was supposedly the inspiration for the character of "All-the-Way Mae" played by pop superstar Madonna in Penny Marshall's blockbuster film, *A League of Their Own*. Salty, opinionated, and a great storyteller, Maybelle Blair tells it like it is with a sparkle in her eye and a song in her heart for her one true love: baseball.

SHIRLEY BURKOVICH–UTILITY

Her nickname was "Hustle," and she came by it honestly. Shirley Burkovich was the personification of a "gamer:" her complete package of skills allowed her to play every position except catcher. She took the field for the Muskegon Lassies, the Springfield Sallies, and the legendary Rockford Peaches. Her stint in the All-American Girls Professional Baseball League brought her a lifetime of experiences before she settled down to a long career with a telephone company.

> *Nearly 70 years later, they cross the country together to promote girls' baseball so that someday they, too, may have "a league of their own." I sat down with this dynamic duo while teenaged girls from Australia and the USA battled it out on a historic baseball field in Anaheim, California. –Jon Leonoudakis*

How did you come to baseball?

MAYBELLE: Well, I came by it naturally because my family was involved in baseball. In fact, I think before I even had anything to drink, I was teething on or sucking on a baseball. My family had a whole team. My father had his brothers and his cousins called

"The Blair Nine." So, I absolutely grew up in a baseball family as they traveled all over Texas and played baseball.

SHIRLEY: I think all of us played with the boys on sandlots and vacant lots and just tried to have something to do for girls at that time. It was just a growing up process for us.

What years are we talking about when you started playing with the boys?

SHIRLEY: Forty, early forties.

Were you accepted?

SHIRLEY: Absolutely, because I was as good as some of the boys.

How did you get drafted into the AAGPBL?

MAYBELLE: I was out playing softball and showing off as I always tried to do. I guess I showed off pretty good that day because a scout from the All-American Girls Professional Baseball League was out there, which I didn't even know there was such a league.

And he says, "I want you to sign a contract to play professional ball."

And I say, "Aw, don't give me that. There isn't any professional baseball [for women]."

And he says, "oh yes, there is, and we pay these guys."

"You're out of your mind," I said. "I don't believe it."

He says, "well, it's true…let me take you home, and I wanna talk to your parents about signing you up to come play ball."

And I say, "there is no way my mother's going let me out of this house and just forget it because I'm telling you right now she's not going to let me out."

He says, "well, let me try." I said, "well, okay, fine. I'd love it."

We went in, and I introduced my parents to him. He started telling them all about the All-American Girls Professional Baseball League. Of course, my folks were looking very suspicious because they knew there wasn't any league, too.

My mother says, "there is no way my daughter is playing any ball. She's not leaving this house."

He says, "Mrs. Blair, you don't understand. We're going to pay her $55 a week, and when she's traveling, we're going to give her traveling expenses."

My mother says, "George, go crank up the car! I'm packing her suitcase. She's going to be leaving here immediately."

So, the next train to Chicago, I was on it. Anyway, that's my story because I was going to make more money than my father was making. And at that time, we needed it.

SHIRLEY: My brother saw an article in the newspaper saying that they were holding tryouts for the AAGPBL.

He said to me, "why don't you go down and try out?"

I said, "No, no. I'm too—don't wanna go down there. Too scared." So, he took the day off of work, and he took me down there.

He said, "we'll just sit in the stands and you can watch—then, see what you think."

We went down, sat in the stands, and I watched everybody out there playing. I think he knew once he got me watching the other girls, there was no way I wasn't going to go down there and try out. And sure enough, I did. Went down there. Tried out. A couple weeks later, I got a telegram saying to report to spring training in Indiana.

My mom said, "what about school?" I was only 16-years-old and I was still in school.

Shirley, with glove, poses with her bat-wielding brother.
(Courtesy Shirley Burkovich)

We went to the principal to see if it would be possible for me to leave in April. School didn't end until June, and this was April. They looked at my grades, of course, and they said, "fine, she can go."

The next problem was my mom saying, "I've never heard of AAGPBL baseball league. I'm going to go down with you."

So, she bought a ticket and went to the spring training site with me and met the manager and the chaperone. Once both assured her that everything was on the up and up, she said I could stay.

How did your nickname of "Hustle" come about?

SHIRLEY: I don't know. I think it's just what I did. I kind of moved around the bases. I moved out in the field and just tried to hustle all the time.

My favorite moment was the day I reported to spring training for the first time. That to me was a thrill of a lifetime. To be able to be with a team. Wear a uniform. Play on a team that was not all boys. A girls' team. That was a big moment for me. Of course, I think the ultimate for not only myself but for the league of our own was when we were recognized as a league by Cooperstown [the National Baseball Hall of Fame].

The women of the AAGPBL were recognized in 1988 by a permanent exhibit at the National Baseball Hall of Fame in Cooperstown, NY. (Photo by Jon Leonoudakis)

MAYBELLE: Well, my very favorite moment was when I first put on the uniform, and I put my cleats on, and I started walking out towards the field, and I could hear the click, click, click, click, click of the feet walking out towards the field. And thought my dream had come true. I am going to be able to play professional baseball. And that's why we're trying so hard today to give these other people the same feeling that we have.

What are your feelings when you hold a baseball?

MAYBELLE: That feeling is the greatest feeling in the whole world. In fact, I could hold a baseball forever less people think I was crazy. I could carry it around with me always. It's just a natural feeling for me to hold a baseball. It's my love. It's my security blanket.

SHIRLEY: I just go back to our playing days. Out there in the field, fielding a grounder with this ball. Catching a fly ball. Watching it hit the bat. Those are memories that come back when you get a baseball in your hand. All those years that you played and had that opportunity.

Who was the toughest pitcher you faced?

Pitcher Jean Faut is regarded as the best pitcher in the history of the AAGPBL. She was 20-2 in 1952 with a 0.93 earned-run average.

(Courtesy of the National Baseball Hall of Fame Library, Cooperstown, NY)

SHIRLEY: Jean Faut. She threw hard, and she was just an all-around player. Not only a pitcher, but she was a good fielder and good hitter or a good sacrifice person.

MAYBELLE: Lois Florreich. She played for the Rockford Peaches. And I'll tell you, you didn't know if it was going to hit you, or kill you, or what. She had a hard fastball and half the time, it wasn't going over the plate. It was coming right at you. And we didn't have any helmets or any form of protection. So, she had me a little nervous. The only one that ever really made me nervous at the plate.

Pitcher Lois "Flash" Florreich went 22-7 with an ERA of 0.67 in 1949.

(Courtesy of the Center for History)

Did you ever get any hits off of her?

MAYBELLE: Oh God, I can't remember.

What was it like for you playing baseball in skirts?

MAYBELLE: Even when we played in skirts, we didn't have any protection. There just wasn't any in those days. You either went out like that or you didn't play. You know, we didn't even think about getting hurt or getting strawberries or anything. That was just natural. If we got one, we got one. They broke a fingernail. We broke a fingernail.

In the old days, ballplayers played hurt. Just like with the Cal Ripken's and the Lou Gehrig's, they kept playing hurt or not, you were out there on the field. And that's the way we were with our skirts.

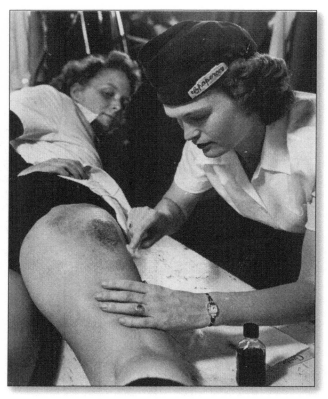

A chaperone tends to a "strawberry"
on the leg of Lois Florreich.
(Courtesy of the Center for History)

SHIRLEY: Yeah, that's true. We played for, as they say, "love of the game." Whether you played in a skirt or shorts or long pants or in a bikini, if you wanted to play, that's what you played in.

Did the unwritten rules of baseball apply when you played?

SHIRLEY: I don't remember that ever being a problem.

MAYBELLE: I don't think we had the problem there.

Nobody out of line? Nobody needed to "get corrected"?

SHIRLEY: I know there were times when a base runner would come flying into home plate and try to upend the catcher. But a lot of the times, that's part of the game. Same as second base on the double play. I mean, that's your job.

MAYBELLE: Yeah, take 'em out. That's what you're running there for. Break that double play up. That's baseball.

SHIRLEY: I don't remember anybody saying, "Hey! Watch it" Or throwing. We weren't the fighting type. We didn't empty dugouts and run onto the field.

You didn't have what they call "benching jockeying?" [a practice of players heckling their opponents]

SHIRLEY: Yeah. Yeah. Oh yeah, we had bench jockeying. But it wasn't malicious, it was just kind of fun.

Why do American women have a problem getting the chance to play baseball?

MAYBELLE: I think that after the war and after our league, a league of their own died, people, the women, were supposed to go back in the house and forget about being "Rosie the Riveter" and being able to play. And men then didn't accept the women.

They thought they couldn't play and they didn't want to even be bothered with it! But the world is changing now, and the girls are getting a little opportunity and getting a little recognition that they can play baseball.

If they love it well enough, why can't we play baseball and have our own leagues again, like the WNBA, and do our thing? We can play baseball, and we want to prove it to people that these girls are great baseball players.

SHIRLEY: I think it is because it's still that baseball is a man's world. People, for some reason, don't want to accept women playing a man's sport, which everyone considers a man's sport. But now they see that these girls can do it, just like you see out here today, the USA team, the Australian team. These girls can play baseball.

We need to realize this, as well as step forward to get together with these girls and start some sort of organization. That's what we're trying to do.

Young Colbie Wolfe is part of a new generation of girls eschewing softball to play baseball.

(Photo by Karl Mondon)

MAYBELLE: My personal belief is that I hope they achieve their dreams like we had our dreams, which is still the best parts of our whole life and our memories is playing baseball because we loved it so well. At that time didn't think we had a chance to play, but for the war. That was the only reason we were able to play ball. So, we're hoping that Major League Baseball will wake up and help us promote women's baseball because we have all of these Double A, Triple A ball diamonds that we can be out there playing on while they're out traveling. The girls are good. Give 'em a chance. That's all we ask.

SHIRLEY: These girls just need to have the opportunity like we had to show the world they can play baseball. Until somebody realizes that and steps forward to help us out, we're going to stay where we are.

MAYBELLE: In fact, we've started a new organization called the International Women's Baseball Center, where we're trying to create the history of women's baseball, which will include way back when it first began up through the time of the All-Americans, which Shirley and I belong to and we're on the board.

Ten-year-old Cameron Ely is the only girl playing in her PONY League program in Valencia, CA.

(Courtesy of Paul Sunde)

What we would like to do is put together a traveling museum where we will go to the Major League baseball stadiums and educate people about women in baseball, which then will help girls to be able to play baseball.

MAYBELLE: Shirley and I just got back from Orlando, Florida as ambassadors for Baseball For All and the IWBC. That was an all-girls tournament down there. And if that wasn't a thrill! There was about oh, ten teams, Shirley?

SHIRLEY: Fourteen teams.

MAYBELLE: Girls from all over the country and Canada. What a thrill that was for us. And what we're trying to do is help promote, create and open the doors for girls in baseball.

SHIRLEY: It was quite a thrill to see these girls playing. A lot of them came up to us and said it was probably the first time that they've ever played in a tournament where they played against girls. When they played in tournaments before, they were always on a boys' team. So, they didn't really have their own.

MAYBELLE: Another thing. Monique Davis made such headlines, which was wonderful for the women. But they don't realize there's hundreds of girls out there as good as Monique… maybe better. But it was wonderful this happened in that Little League World Series, that they went that far, because we do have many, many, many Davis's playing ball.

What's been the biggest change in baseball in your time?

MAYBELLE: The helmets. This protector. That protector. Sliding pads. Knee protectors. Toe protectors. They look like a knight running down to first base, they got so many protectors on. This is what I have to laugh about; mostly is all the protection that they have, which is good. Don't get me wrong. We needed it too.

But we went out there and played in dresses. No sliding pads. And we came up with strawberries that I'm still digging dirt out of my side. I can't even wear hose sometimes, because they get stuck and then the run goes down my leg!

Slides like these led to "strawberries" for women of the AAGPBL. (Courtesy National Baseball Hall of Fame Library, Cooperstown, NY)

SHIRLEY: You know, I'm a purist in baseball. I like the olden days. I like when we had two leagues; the American League, the National League, and the two divisions.

Then we had eight teams in each division. They didn't play the other league until the World Series. That's what I like. I realize now that there's money involved.

But still, I like the olden days when the American League and the National League were two separate leagues. There was no inter-league play. There was no designated hitter.

How did you feel when aluminum bats came in?

MAYBELLE: Oh, don't even ask me about aluminum bats. There's only one bat, and that's a wood bat. I love it. Give me a Louisville Slugger any day of my life, and I'm ready to go. But you hear that "ping" or "ting" or whatever it is against that aluminum bat. And it gives them all that extra oomph. They should be playing with wooden bats at all times, I think.

[former MLB pitcher] Bill "Spaceman" Lee says using a wood bat will make you a better person.

MAYBELLE: Yeah, and old Bill's right. His aunt, Annabelle Lee was my roommate. She taught him how to pitch.

What's one rule you'd like to see changed in baseball?

SHIRLEY: The DH [designated hitter] rule is—
MAYBELLE: Yeah, that bugs everybody.
SHIRLEY: I can see where it's prolonged careers for a lot of players

that DH rule. But, still, the pitcher's part of the nine starting players. So, he should have to bat too.

MAYBELLE: Absolutely. I agree with that a hundred percent. That's the old-time baseball. Shirley and my generation, it's hard for us to even think about having the designated hitter.

Just like with infield practice. We like to watch infield. Infield practice to me is the most wonderful thing in the world. You can see how they handle themselves around the base or how they go after a ball. How they throw. Can they go to the left? Can they go to the right? It's just poetry in motion. I think the fans should be able to watch infield practice.

SHIRLEY: Getting back to the pitchers...this is a time where pitchers should be practicing sacrificing. Bunting. I have never seen such poor bunting as I see in the Major Leagues today. I don't know who their teachers were, but if we ever bunted like that, we'd be on the bench in no time. That's their job in the National League...to sacrifice, usually. You have a couple of good-hitting pitchers. But nine out of ten of them are up there to sacrifice. If you can't lay down a bunt, then something's wrong.

MAYBELLE: Bruce Bochy, he is doing such a magnificent job with San Francisco Giants without a lot of talent. He's playing hustle baseball; they're running, using the hit and run and stealing bases. Oh, it's just fun to watch 'em.

SHIRLEY: I was just going to say a lot of teams depend on the home run for their runs rather than like you say. Bunting, hit and run, moving the runner, hitting the opposite field to move the runner. You don't see a lot of that anymore. Fundamental baseball.

Complete this sentence for me: "Baseball is..."

SHIRLEY: Baseball is my passion. Something I will love for the rest of my life and I hope that we'll have the same opportunity for these other girls to play that I had.

MAYBELLE: Baseball is the healthiest sport in the whole world. To me, it is a whole lifetime of happiness and looking forward to happiness for all these younger girls to be able to go out and experience the fun and the joy I have had playing baseball. Give 'em the opportunity.

What do you like about today's game?

SHIRLEY: Well, I just like baseball. I watch anybody who's on TV. Whatever game's on, I'll watch even though it's not my favorite team or whatever. When you love something as much as we love baseball, it never gets out of your system. It's always there. Always that passion to watch or even, I'd like some time to just get out and throw a few.

Do you still get out there and throw the ball?

SHIRLEY: Well, I guess I could. I don't very often. There's not many people around, except people like Maybelle, that are still able to catch a ball.

MAYBELLE: Yeah, we can still throw it around pretty good… we can still give it the old rooty-tooty, you know. No problem. We just can't move!

How many players are left from the All-American Girls Professional Baseball League?

MAYBELLE: Oh, we love the reunions. Absolutely love 'em. Gosh, Shirley and I have promoted what, four reunions?

SHIRLEY: Yes.

MAYBELLE: One year, we went on a cruise. And it was just a great, great time. It's good to see our old friends again. We're down to, I don't know, I'm guessing maybe 115, that's still active, right?

SHIRLEY: Yeah.

MAYBELLE: Maybe a little less now. I don't know for sure. We're losing 'em like flies because we're getting so old. So, we gotta make hay while the sun shines. We try to meet every year, and next year it'll be in Florida.

Baseball has opened many doors for you, hasn't it?

MAYBELLE: Oh, absolutely. It has opened so many doors not only for our enjoyment but for other peoples' enjoyment. Kids get a big kick out of us coming out and being with them. These are things that we enjoy. We want to encourage people to help promote women's baseball.

SHIRLEY: We owe a lot of gratitude to Penny Marshall for telling our story. Had it not been for that movie [*A League of Their Own*], we would have still been in obscurity because nobody knew about our league unless you lived in that part of the country. We have her to thank for getting that movie out and showing the way it was at that time.

If you could share a message two hundred years from now about baseball, what would it be?

MAYBELLE: I hope that you have the same opportunities and the passion and the love for the game that we have and that you will have the thrills and joys of baseball.

SHIRLEY: I hope there's a league of their own.

Shirley played for the Fort Wayne Daisies in 1950. (Courtesy of the Center of History)

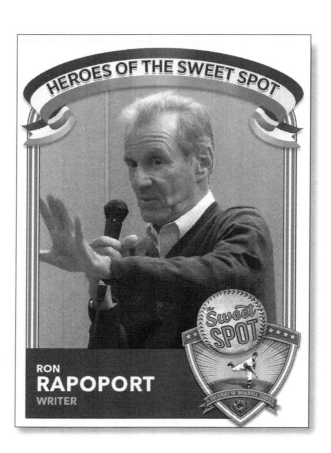

HEROES OF THE SWEET SPOT

RON
RAPOPORT
WRITER

RON RAPOPORT

"Baseball is the tie that binds. It binds generations. It binds families. It binds historians."

Ron Rapoport is a writer, journalist, and author who, in a career that spanned five decades, wrote for the Chicago Sun-Times and the Los Angeles Times and provided sports commentary for National Public Radio. He continues to write books about sports and show business. In 1972, Ron was covering baseball for the Los Angeles Times when Jackie Robinson came to town for the retiring of his number at Dodger Stadium. Ron's interview with Jackie would be one of the last he gave before his death a few months later. The breadth and extent of Ron's career and interests will fascinate fans of baseball, American culture, and history. We at the Sweet Spot celebrate writers like Ron, who document sports and culture with style and perspective that never grows old.

I WAS BORN IN DETROIT, MICHIGAN but as a sportswriter, author and sports columnist, I've worked in Chicago and Los Angeles most of my life.

I grew up as a Detroit Tigers fan in one of their misbegotten last-place eras, back in the 40s and early 50s. I started writing sports for my high school paper, and I loved it. My joke is that I knew what I wanted to be when I was 14 years old, and I never grew up.

I was a fan as a kid, but covering sports as a living quickly takes the fan out of you. You understand that your approach to the game is not hoping that somebody will win or somebody will lose, but that you'll get a good story. You relate to it totally differently. You're rooting for the story. You're rooting for yourself.

When I grew up in Detroit, there was a columnist named Doc Greene who was a very literate guy, in the mold of writers like Red Smith and Jimmy Cannon, whom I would discover later.

When I went to Stanford, I started reading the San Francisco papers. Candlestick Park was just being built, Willie Mays was still playing for the Giants, and it was interesting to see another team, read the writers who covered them, and watch the fans who rooted for them on the other side of the country.

When I left college, I went to work for the late, lamented *Minneapolis Star*. It was big and fat afternoon paper, full of ads, while the *Minneapolis Tribune*, which survives today, was the intellectual lost leader, owned by the same company. The *Tribune* was a morning paper, didn't have a lot of ads, which shows you how much the newspaper business has changed. After I left Minneapolis, I went to New York to work for *Sport* magazine as an editor, but I wanted to get back into writing, so I went to the Associated Press, where I worked on city side for a while, running around town with a pocket full of dimes and calling in stories to the rewrite desk. As I said, another era.

I worked for two years at 50 Rockefeller Plaza in New York, then I went to San Francisco for two years where I was the entire sports staff. I covered everything myself. The Bay Area had two baseball teams, two football teams, two major-college teams, a hockey team, a basketball team, and a small-college conference. That was a test of my skill and daring and I learned to write quickly because that's what the wire services demanded.

Then I came to *Los Angeles Times*, where I covered the Angels and the Dodgers for a few years and then becoming a sort of jack-of-all-trades. I covered UCLA basketball in the John Wooden era, the Rams, the Lakers and other teams and I wrote a lot of features. The *Times* would run a 2,500-word feature every single day in the sports section—it sounds amazing, doesn't it?—and I wrote my share of them.

Jim Murray was working at the *Times* then and he was kind of a god to all of us because he was reinventing sports writing by writing about them in a different kind of way than anybody else had done before. John Hall wrote a note-column for the *Los Angeles Times* then and to this day, I maintain he's the best sports notes writer I ever read.

Then I moved to Chicago where I became a columnist for the *Sun-Times.* I stayed there from 1977 to 1988, left and came back to Los Angeles, this time at the *LA Daily News* in the San Fernando Valley where I wrote a column for eight years. Then I went back to the *Chicago Sun-Times* and stayed there for another eight years. This is a typical sportswriter's resume of that time, I think. We moved around a lot. In 2006, I came back to California, where I am "retired," but I really haven't stopped working on one project or another. It's more than a decade now and I have never not had a project in the pipeline, mostly books now.

What is a "newspaperman?"

A newspaperman is a dying breed now because newspapers are dying. We've all had to learn how to accommodate ourselves to changing technology. When I broke in, we would carry an Olivetti typewriter, a little green thing in a green case. Sometimes, we would call in our stories, sometimes dictate them, and later send them in on a telecopier, which contained a drum that you would attach a piece of paper to and clamp it in place, which was attached to a telephone. An arrow would move down the page, transmitting at six minutes for a page. What we would have done for a fax machine. It came in Samsonite luggage, which we checked as baggage on planes. So here we were, carrying a typewriter and a telecopier, which together weighed more than 20 pounds.

In the late 70s, computers started coming in and we went through every iteration of the portable computer. The first one didn't have a memory. If you were in a cramped press box and somebody walked by and kicked your plug out, your story was gone. Then there were several others where you plugged the phone in directly.

Finally, RadioShack, bless their hearts, brought in a very small computer that ran on four AA batteries, which allowed us to write on airplanes. The only downside was it had a very small screen and you could only see four lines of type, about 40 words, at a time. We got used to it, though, and we used them for ten years until finally, modern laptops came along. We were the guinea-pig generation, starting with typewriters, which I will bring into journalism classes to show students, who have never seen them before, and moving through every kind of portable computer.

Today, the biggest problem covering the team on a day-to-day basis for newspapers is one of time. The games last later and later all the time and the deadlines get earlier and earlier all the time. It's the same problem we had 40 years ago, but it's much more difficult now because anybody can log on to the internet or turn on the TV and get the latest story. What is a poor newspaperman supposed to do? He doesn't have time to catch his breath, but he has to make it new and interesting and different from what the digital people and the television people have already done.

How did the interview with Jackie Robinson come about?

It was 1972 in June, and the Dodgers were retiring their first numbers in Los Angeles. They chose well. Sandy Koufax, Roy Campanella, and Jackie Robinson. You can't do better than that.

(Courtesy National Baseball Hall of Fame, Cooperstown, NY)

Jackie did not go to Old-Timers' games. His falling out with baseball in general, and the Dodgers in particular, was long-lasting, and he didn't care much about baseball. He had negative feelings about the game. He thought that it hadn't conquered its racism and he was upset there were no black managers.

Jackie was feisty to the end. He did not mellow as he grew older. But when they called him and said, "We're retiring your number, Sandy and Roy are going to be there, too." He felt he couldn't say no. One of the reasons he came was that Gil Hodges had just died at an early age. Jackie said that he thought he would be the first of the "Boys of Summer" to go and it hit him hard when Hodges died.

So, Jackie came out to Los Angeles—I was covering baseball for the *Times* then—and what struck me was, no notice was taken of his presence. No press conference was called. No fuss was made about his being in town. It was the 25th anniversary of the integration of baseball, of his joining the Dodgers, and nobody said anything about it. If you jump ahead 25 years to the 50th anniversary, and the great ceremony that accompanied that, you'll understand my surprise.

I called the Dodgers, and I said, "Are you doing anything with Jackie?"

They said, "No. He's staying at the Biltmore. You can call him there if you want."

I called the Biltmore and I said, "Can I talk to Jackie Robinson?"

The operator said, "Wait just a minute, I'll connect you."

The next voice I heard was Jackie's. I was a little taken aback. You mean anybody can just call in off the street—they didn't ask me to identify myself—and talk to Jackie Robinson?

I tried to recover my wits and said, "Mr. Robinson, I work for the LA Times. Can I come see you sometime when it's convenient?"

He said, "Come on over now."

I went to the Biltmore, and my confusion grew stronger when I opened the door to a very small room. No suite for Jackie Robinson, just a room with a bed in it. The lights were off, and he was in bed, under the covers, in the middle of the afternoon. He was gray-haired, very heavy, had suffered a heart attack and was almost blind. What made it especially difficult for me was that the man in that bed and under those covers, in the middle of the afternoon was 53 years old. He was the greatest athlete of our time—baseball, basketball, football, track, there was nothing he didn't excel at—and he was in terrible shape.

He said, "Here, let me switch the light on for you so you can take notes."

We talked for an hour, and he talked about everything. He talked about Walter O'Malley. He talked about the reasons for his falling out with baseball. He talked about what it had been like breaking into baseball. He talked about playing for Leo Durocher. He went on and on and I couldn't take notes fast enough.

Finally, an hour later, I could see he needed his rest and got ready to leave. But before leaving, I asked him a question I had not prepared. It was a question I've never asked a sports figure before, and I never expect to ask again.

"Have you considered your place in history?" I said.

He gave me a very eloquent answer, saying that he was proud of what he'd done, he hoped maybe he had had some kind of an influence, but no, he didn't really consider himself the same category as a Martin Luther King.

I said goodbye, wrote my story, which the *Times* bannered across the top of the page of the Sunday paper sports section—about as good as I can go.

Now, it's the day of the retirement ceremonies and out on the field, Jackie is being led around by somebody because he couldn't see well. It's batting practice, the usual chatter is going on, Koufax is there, Campanella is in his wheelchair. It's all very convivial.

Suddenly, from the stands near home plate, a little bit down towards the third base line, a middle-aged man yells out, "Mr. Robinson! Mr. Robinson! Will you sign my ball for me, please?"

Jackie turns around and looks at him, and the guy softly underhands the baseball right at Jackie.

Anyone could have caught it. A five-year-old boy could have caught it. But Jackie didn't see it and the ball hit him in the head, hurt him.

The guy sees what he's done and he says, "Oh, my God! I'm so sorry. I'm so sorry. I'm so sorry."

They led Jackie away and though he was in pain, he turned out to be OK. That was my last sight of him.

Postscript. In my article, I write I had interviewed Peter O'Malley, who'd given me his side of why he thought Jackie had this falling out with his father. I also interviewed Don Newcombe, Jackie's old teammate who worked for the Dodgers in community relations, who had been partly responsible for getting Jackie to come to town. Don told me he thought Jackie regretted his estrangement from baseball and was glad to come to Dodger Stadium.

A week later, I was shocked to find a letter from Jackie Robinson in my mailbox at the *Times*.

My article was OK, he said, but "That story Don Newcombe told you is a bunch of crap. He's been trying to peddle that crap about me regretting being estranged from baseball for years, it's not true. I don't regret anything."

A couple of months later at the World Series, they made the big mistake of putting Jackie on television. He was glad to be there he said, but he wouldn't be satisfied until he could look across that diamond and see a black man managing a team in the major leagues. He died about a month later.

That's my Jackie Robinson story.

◆◆◆

What was it like writing in a sports-crazy town like Chicago?

People in New York or Boston or Philadelphia might disagree with me, but I think that the Chicago fan is a breed apart. Sports is almost a religion there. It starts with the two baseball teams. "I'm a Sox fan because my father was a Sox fan and his father was a Sox fan." They refer to the marriage between a Sox fan and a Cubs fan as a mixed marriage. So, covering baseball in Chicago was exhilarating because you knew you were writing for an audience that cared so much.

Becoming a columnist changes the equation for any writer who makes that transition. All of a sudden, your name is in large type or maybe your picture is in the paper. It's kind of like an actor seeing his name on a marquee for the first time. It's exciting, but it's also kind of scary, especially in the beginning, because you have to decide how to handle it. Do you want to be an "I" columnist, writing in the first-person singular all the time? Are you going to try to be funny? Are you going to try to be outrageous? Are you going to try to write the water-cooler column that everybody's talking about the next day? Do you want to take a break once in a while to write what they used to call the rainy-day column, which is something away from the beat? You have decisions to make that you never had when you were covering a beat or getting assignments from the sports editor.

The smartest thing I ever read about being a columnist, came from Russell Baker, the political columnist for the *New York Times*.

He said, "A columnist spends his first year finding his voice and the rest of his career fighting it."

I talked to Jim Murray about being a columnist once. I said, "Jeez, it's like every January, it's the Super Bowl, and then every February, it's spring training. Every March, it's the Final Four, and so on. After a while, you kind of meet yourself coming around corners. Jim, the world of sports is finite, isn't it?"

Jim said, "Yeah, and so am I."

You got to know Ernie Banks after his retirement. What was he really like?

Ernie had a certain reputation that everybody knew: Mr. Sunshine. "Let's play two. It's a beautiful day for a ballgame. How's your wife?" Very sunny. Very optimistic. But when you think about it, it's no surprise that there was a serious side to Ernie. I mean, how could there not be?

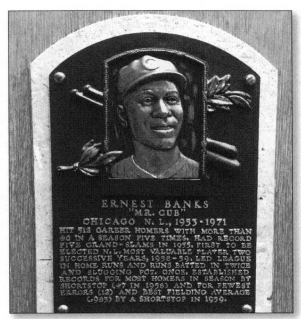

Ernie's plaque in the Baseball Hall of Fame

What I learned was that in a public setting, after about 20 minutes of, "How are you doing? Isn't it grand to be alive on a beautiful day like today?" his voice would become lower and he would begin to talk about serious things. I also learned that if I got him away from the public in his home in Marina del Rey, we could sit down and talk about serious things right away. I learned that the most important thing to know about Ernie was that he was what he seemed, but he was much more, too.

We had long conversations, about his early days growing up in Dallas, about his family, about the Negro Leagues and on and on through his life and career. I knew Ernie best in the last 10 or 12 years of his life as he got older and became more frail. But he was still fine upstairs. He had a photographic memory. He'd remember meeting somebody and who their family was five years later.

Ernie asked me if I would help him write his autobiography. He had been working on one with another writer who had died and he asked if I wanted to take over.

Ernie's retired number flag flies over Wrigley Field
(Photo by Lorena Petani)

I said, "Sure," and I brought him a contract from a publisher and we started talking. Then he decided he didn't want to do it after all.

A year or so later, he called me again and said, "What about the book?" so we started doing it again. Then he pulled out again. All in all, we had about 10 hours on tape, which I'm using as the basis for the biography I'm writing of him. I've talked to more than 100 people who knew Ernie—his family, his teammates, people who worked for the Cubs during his era and many more. I think the book will help people understand that Ernie was a far more interesting and complicated man than the image that was attached to him throughout his life.

◆◆◆

The big difference between Cubs and White Sox fans is that White Sox fans resent Cub fans, resent the cute little Cubby image—their adorable ballpark and their adorable logo and their adorable losing streak and curses and so on.

Wrigley Field opened in 1914 and is one of baseball's hallowed cathedrals. (Photo by Lorena Petani)

The White Sox played in Comiskey Park, which was a nice old ball park, but not as charming. Now, they're in a great big monstrosity of a new ball field that can't compare to Wrigley Field. They feel that they don't get their due, that the papers and the media are more interested in the Cubs. They might be right. But if White Sox fans don't like Cubs fans, Cubs fans don't care much. They don't pay much attention and that gets White Sox fans mad all over again.

When Bill Veeck owned the White Sox, he once took a ruler to the *Chicago Tribune's* coverage of the White Sox and the Cubs over a period of time and said that the Cubs had many more column inches than the White Sox. It wasn't true, but it made for a typical Bill Veeck story

You worked in Chicago when some colorful sportscasters dominated the scene. Who was the most memorable?

Harry Caray was inescapable when he was broadcasting the Sox and then the Cubs. Did he butcher players' names? He did. Could he not see very well at the end? He couldn't. Was he not the most reliable announcer, especially at the end? He was not. Did it matter? It did not. You couldn't stop watching or listening. He was just always saying crazy things.

He was politically incorrect. The Cubs had a ball girl, Marla Collins, and he would almost salivate about her over the airways. Mark Grace was dating Janine Turner who was in the TV Show *Northern Exposure* at the time, and when she would come in to visit him, they would turn the camera on her and Harry would practically proposition her on the air. It was just unbelievable, but he was so funny about it.

I liked being around Kenny "Hawk" Harrelson. I don't think I would be insulting him if I said he was the biggest homer I ever saw in the history of baseball. I mean, it's the good guys and the bad guys. It's us and them. He wasn't Harry—nobody was—but it was fun to listen to, too.

I had no sooner started writing a column in Chicago when I interviewed Jimmy Piersall. He said, "You know, going crazy was the best thing that ever happened to me."

It hit all the wire services. It was in *Time* magazine. Jimmy was another guy who didn't care what he said and didn't care what anybody thought of what he said.

There was a time when Harry Caray was doing a play-by-play for the White Sox and Jimmy was doing the color. They were feuding with Bill Veeck. If you can imagine this, the announcers were feuding with the owner who paid them. They might say something ripping their own team, their own players.

Harry was saying bad things about Tony LaRussa, who was just beginning his career as a manager. It ended up with a fight in the bar and it got to the point where the *Sun-Times* had to monitor the broadcasts because you never knew if Harry and Jimmy were going to say something so outrageous you had to put in the paper.

What was your experience as a Hall of Fame voter?

2016 was my last year with a Hall of Fame vote. It was supposed to be lifetime for baseball writers, but now, they've changed it to 10 years after you last covered baseball. A lot of writers were upset about this, but I didn't mind that much. When I was writing a column, voting for the Hall of Fame was always good for a column or two every year.

There are two problems with the Hall of Fame. One is, it takes three-quarters of the vote to get in. You'd never have a president, you'd never have a pope if you needed 75%.

Then there is the electorate, the writers who have different ideas about who should get in. There are some people who think nobody, not Mickey Mantle, not Ted Williams, not Babe Ruth, belongs in on the first ballot. They just won't vote for anybody on the first ballot. That's why there has never been a unanimous selection of the Hall of Fame.

Then you have people that think only the best of the best should get in. Only Ted Williams and Mickey Mantle and Sandy Koufax and Ernie Banks. Then there are people, like me, who take a broader view and think that if you were a great player in your era, that if your numbers were great, that if your contribution was great, and if your team couldn't have won without you, then you belong in.

You're allowed to vote for ten people and some people say, "I always vote for ten," and others say, "I only vote for the ones I think should be in that year."

The first year that the steroid guys appeared on the ballot—we're talking Barry Bonds, Roger Clemons, Sammy Sosa, Rafael Palmeiro, Mark McGwire—I voted for them all. I wrote a column explaining why and the next thing you know, I get a call from MLB wanting me to go on their television network to explain myself. My position is this: I'm not defending their use of steroids. I'm not saying they didn't break the rules. But if you're going to ignore them, you're going to write off an entire generation of baseball. You're going to ignore all of the excitement and all of the things they brought to the game. I don't see how you can do that. Yes, you've got to try to control steroids. Yes, you've got to try to make everybody play by the same rules. On the other hand, you can't wave it away with a magic wand.

So, I explained myself on MLB TV and they treated me nicely. They said it was an interesting position. Then they said that the guy who'd been on before me said he had only voted for Dale Murphy because he was the only guy on the ballot who he personally knew and liked.

I said to myself, "My ballot's no more outrageous than his."

I voted for Pete Rose, too. You had to write him in because his name wasn't on the ballot. At least, Bonds and McGwire and Clemens and the rest of them had their names on the ballot. Pete did not. I think it's outrageous that he's not in the Hall of Fame.

Did he bet on the games? Yes. Did he lie about betting on games? Yes. Was he one of the greatest players of his generation? Yes. Did he love baseball more than anything else? Yes. Did he do more to promote baseball than any player of his era? Yes. Would he talk to any writer without asking, "Are you from *Sports Illustrated* or *The New York Times?*" Yes.

Pete lived and breathed that game. I think it's outrageous that he's not in, but it's obviously never going to happen in my lifetime.

What do you like about baseball?

Baseball is the tie that binds. It binds generations. It binds families. It binds historians. You can go back so far. I was researching a collection of Ring Lardner's journalism a few years ago and it took me back into the early 1900s and the 20s and the 30s. You can see the generations pile one on top of the other. The game has fallen out of fashion a little because football and basketball move much faster and have taken over. But there will always be a place for baseball, for the quieter, more contemplative aspect of it.

It amuses me that all of a sudden, they've decided World Series and playoff games go on too long and they're trying to get the pitcher to pitch faster and they use a clock. What they don't mention is that they have three minutes between innings for commercials. That's what makes the games last so long.

And because there is so much money involved, television can tell baseball what to do because they're paying the bills. For instance, I am still waiting for the first interview of a manager in a dugout while the game is going to tell me something important or useful.

What I find myself doing more and more is just concentrating on the games. The athletes are better than ever. The games are better than ever. If you separate it from all the silliness that's going around before and during and after, and just concentrate on the games and the athletes themselves, it's wonderful.

What's your take on the bat-flipping in the game today?

I'm okay with the entertainment aspect of it. I don't mind bat-flipping and admiring home runs. I don't mind a pitcher pumping his fist after a big strikeout. But I do think a batter who flips his bat and stands there to admire it might not have too much of a complaint if he gets brushed back the next time up.

Back in the 1960s, the bleacher bums in Wrigley Field used to throw hot dogs out on the field at Pete Rose because they thought he made easy catches look difficult and was so flashy. Pete being Pete, would pick a hot dog up and pretend to eat it.

You reported on the Angels in the 70s when Nolan Ryan became one of the most dominant pitchers in the history of the game. What stands out about him?

I covered Nolan Ryan's first two no-hitters. I saw the beast get out of the cage. Nolan was something; he pitched his first no-hitter in May 1973, in Kansas City, and another one in July in Detroit. The Detroit game was where at the end, Norm Cash came up carrying a table leg as if to say he had as much chance of hitting Ryan with it as with a baseball bat. It was the best-pitched game I ever saw. He struck out 17 Tigers while pitching a no-hitter.

I remember there was a story, perhaps apocryphal, where they asked a hitter what he thought of when he was going up to face Nolan Ryan and he said, "My wife and kids."

Players would get "Ryanitis" when they knew he was pitching. They would somehow not be available for the days when he was on the mound. Willie Mays, in particular, didn't like hitting against Nolan. He would take a day off when he was pitching.

Which players stood out when you covered the Dodgers in the 70s and 80s?

Tommy John was a wonderful guy, very self-deprecating. I covered him with the Dodgers and it was great to see him win more games after the surgery that bears his name than before he was injured. Sometimes, I thought he would pitch forever. He would make jokes about it. He would say, "I asked the doctor to give me a Koufax fastball. He gave me a Mrs. Koufax fastball."

And to his credit, Tommy would say they really should call it Frank Jobe surgery. He was just the guy who happened to be the first man to receive it. It was Frank Jobe who invented it. That tells you all you need to know about Tommy.

I covered the Dodgers for the *Los Angeles Daily News* in 1988. During the first game of the World Series, we were all sitting up in the press box, writing our stories, which were focused on the dent that Jose Canseco put in the camera in center field when he hit a home run to put the Oakland A's ahead. Now it's late in the game and we're looking at our watches. We've got to get our stories in. Dennis Eckersley is pitching and nobody's going to get to him so we're feeling good about it, but all of a sudden, he walks a guy, then another guy gets on, and here comes Kirk Gibson.

We're all looking up from our computers as Kirk hits his homer and the stadium erupts. What I notice then and what you will see if you watch the video of his home run, is brake lights in the parking lot. Everybody who just knew the A's were going to win were trying to beat the traffic out of the Dodger Stadium parking lot.

I'm sitting here, thinking to myself, "What would you tell people if you said, 'I went to that game and I missed the home run at the end.'? (laughs) Would you lie about it?"

Anyway, Kirk hits the home run and every word we've written is now vapor on our computers. What are we going to do?! We battle our way through the crowd. We make our way to the elevator. We go into this trainer's room off the Dodger clubhouse where they bring in people for big interviews.

And Kirk is waiting for us. He's got one foot up on the stool. For five minutes, nobody says a word except Kirk, who takes us through it. "I'm in the clubhouse. I hear Vin Scully say something about Gibson not being able to play today. I said, 'Horseshit!' I go hit some balls off a tee. I send word to Tommy to please tell him I can play." Then he goes pitch by pitch through his at-bat. What he's thinking. What he's seeing. Hitting the home run. Waiting for the back-door slider he knows is coming. Running around the bases. Pumping his arm. The works.

We all run upstairs, write as fast as we can, get the story in, take a breath and say, "Thank God for Kirk Gibson." As far as I'm concerned, he performed two miracles that day (laughs), one for Dodgers and one for the poor scribes who had to write about it.

◆◆◆

When you hold that baseball in your hand, what do your heart and soul say?

Well, I guess I would think this little thing here has seen a lot, hasn't it? It's seen the Black Sox, the Babe, the integration of baseball, which took place before the Army was integrated, before the schools were integrated.

It's seen strikes and lockouts when it disappeared for a while and then came back. It's seen the steroid era, the big money era with players making 10, 20, 30, million dollars after one or two good years whereas not long ago even the best players had jobs in the off season to make ends meet. It's been through a lot, seen a lot, yes. But it holds up pretty well. Looks pretty good, doesn't it?

Send a message to baseball fans in 2116, a hundred years from now.

I hope they enjoy it as much as we do. I hope it's still recognizable, that they haven't bent it out of shape too much. I'm afraid that somebody may figure out a way to make it more hip, more with it over a period of 100 years. I hope they don't.

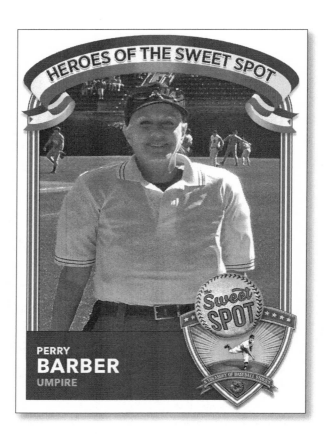

HEROES OF THE SWEET SPOT

PERRY
BARBER
UMPIRE

PERRY BARBER

"Baseball is a way to express my love for life.
It's a gift that I try to give back to other people."

She started out as a singer-songwriter who ended up opening for
the likes of Hall & Oates and Bruce Springsteen. When her interest
flagged, her mother suggested a career in umpiring. Nearly forty
years later, Perry Barber and her well-worn shin guards have
traveled the world, calling baseball games for pros and amateurs
alike. While diminutive in stature, Perry is a giant in her field,
fording streams of ignorance and misogyny to excel as an arbiter
of the game.

I WENT TO PRIVATE SCHOOL WITH my twin sister in New
York City. My mother was very involved in society functions, debutante cotillions, and the Brick Church. We went to
dancing school and saw Nureyev dancing at Lincoln Center.
So, she was very into cultural and educational opportunities
that are available to people in New York.

We partook of as many of them as humanly possible and became
debutantes at her request. I was a debutante with Vera Wang and
Nikki Finke also, who has carved out a very highfalutin' niche
for herself among Hollywood reporters. We had quite a class
of debutantes.

Perry (right), with her sister Warren at their cotillion

How did you come to baseball?

There was nothing in my background or my youth or even my teenage years that would have led anybody to believe that I would wind up as an umpire. And yet I did because I had an interest in trivia from the time *Jeopardy* came on the air in 1963 when my sister and I were ten. We played sick and stayed home the first week so that we could watch it. [later in life, Perry appeared on *Jeopardy* and was a champion]

But it was my interest in trivia that led me to want to beat a friend of mine at baseball trivia. And since I didn't know anything about baseball or baseball trivia, I just decided to educate myself. I went to the bookstore on Fifth Avenue and picked out a few books, and within 24 hours, I was completely hooked on baseball as a history subject. Not as a spectacle to see or participate in, but to read about as if it was history or social studies.

That's how I came by my love for baseball, by learning about the characters and the history and the lore. It took me about a year before I started going to see games. When I did, I was like everybody else. The umpires were kind of there, but not important until they did something wrong. And yet, I met an umpire along the way. His name was Ed Montague, and he made a very big impression on me.

Perry with Ed Montague at Moscone Park,
San Francisco, California

I wrote a song about him because, at that point, I was still a singer-songwriter. I had left college and gone back to New York and became a musician and played mostly solo. Just myself and my guitar. But I did wind up playing with a few bands here and there and had a great career as a performer. Not as a recording artist. I did some demos, but I never really did a lot of recording.

Mostly performing. At the tail end in my mid-twenties, I came upon baseball through my love of trivia. I did wind up beating my friend eventually at baseball trivia, I'm happy to say. And it was my mother who suggested to me that I start umpiring. I don't know if it's something that I ever would have thought of doing myself if she had not suggested it to me.

She put a few things together that I didn't notice about myself. I had written a song about an umpire. I had read a book about an umpire that she saw me reading, and I had this incredible brand new love for baseball.

Because the baseball strike of the summer of 1981 was looming on the horizon, the more I thought about it, the more it seemed a good way to have a physical attachment to the game that I was beginning to need like an addiction.

So, I signed on to umpire this Little League in Indio, California, and inflated my credentials ridiculously to get the job. I guess they were very desperate because they hired not only me but several weeks after I started working, they hired my twin sister to be my partner because there weren't a whole lot of other umpires that were exactly leaping at the chance to work with me back then!

It was more along the lines of, "I'm not going to work with *her!*" When I would walk out on the field, it's like, "is *she* going to umpire?"

But I quickly learned that I wasn't out there to make friends. I was out there to do the best I could. And with my limited knowledge and experience, I made the most of that summer. Luckily, there were one or two umpires that were willing to help me with positioning and knowledge of what to do and how to handle myself out there.

The next January, my twin sister and I went to umpire school. From there, I just kept going, and here I am, thirty-five years later!

I never thought of it as a political statement. It was just that I loved baseball so much and I wanted to be a part of it at that point. Reading about it didn't satisfy that need anymore, although, I was still reading and learning everything I could.

Perry (left) with sister Warren and Harry
Wendelstedt (right) at umpire school

I knew I needed something to fill that gap, and the minute that my mother said, "umpiring" my first reaction was, "are you out of your mind?" But then, the more I thought about it, the more it seemed just a sensible way to get that thing that I needed from baseball, which was to be a physical part of what was going on in the baseball universe, to feel those emotions, to get that rush of adrenalin.

You need a lot of focus, either as a ballplayer and especially as an umpire because you cannot let up for one instant out there or you'll miss something. Something as simple as a pitcher making a little twitch on the mound that could mean the difference between balking in a run and that being the winning run or missing it and thereby having an effect on the outcome of the game, which is something no umpire ever wants to do.

Our role is to be the fair witness and to keep the game flowing, to maintain the flow of the game, too, so, that everybody is a part of the sort of the existential everything-ness of baseball. Of being out there in the sunshine with the breeze and the green grass and the noises and the joy and the happiness, and the disappointment and the success and the failure. It's just such an amazing thing being out there.

That's what I began to need. As I said, it's almost like an addiction. Otherwise, why would I be here, thirty-five years later?! I'm not doing this for the money or the glory. I do it because I still love it. I still find as much stimulation and reward in it as I did the very first day I walked on the field and confronted a lot of people who were very hostile towards me, which was a very new experience.

Because up until then, everything I had done in my life, I had been praised for because I did it well. I was always good in school. My sister and I were debutantes. We were looked up to by our peers. We were talented. People liked us. I very rarely was confronted with hostility or outright enmity directed towards me just because of what I did or what I had become.

Luckily for me, I was brought up, educated and surrounded by strong female mentors and people, women that I could look up to. Starting with my mother and then teachers. My sister and I went to an all-girls school until we were in college.

All of my examples of strength and resolve were women. I was very lucky that I brought that with me when I started umpiring because otherwise, it would have been a lot less fun. It's not easy to understand that the hostility that's directed towards me on the field is a temporary thing. Because even though it is, it still hurts.

And learning how to deal with that; to process the hurtful part of it, so that it doesn't affect my focus or intelligence or experience that I bring to bear as an umpire. How I make my calls or how I deal with the people on the field, which is a very important element of a baseball game that a lot of people don't understand. It's not just accuracy and calling balls and strikes, safe and out, fair or foul.

It's how an umpire handles him or herself. How we relate to the managers, the coaches, and the players. And how we allow them to play the game without making them think that we're there to insert our personality into everything. That's not what I do, and I think it's what most umpires don't do or don't want to do. We just want to be part of the scenery and make everything better; to allow that flow to continue from start to finish, without a lot of blips and bumps along the way.

Ejections and arguments and all of that. You know, it may be entertaining for a little while, but it does detract from the flow of the game. So, we learn early on to be conductors rather than bosses. And I'm not a boss out there. I'm a conductor.

◆ ◆ ◆

I started in Little League, and five years later, I found myself on a major league spring training field. A lot of that was through hard work and dedication and not taking no for an answer and just plowing ahead. No matter what people told me about how foolish I was, it was never going happen, and why was I doing it? And even from some partners that I worked with, I got a lot of hostility and lack of support.

But I got enough that I kept going and I was very fortunate. I remember I left umpire school in the middle of the very last night of school. I took a bus to St. Petersburg because I had gotten per-mission from the director of the Mets fantasy camp, which at that time was taking place in St. Petersburg, to audition for a job as an umpire at the fantasy camp.

I had called two or three other fantasy camp directors. Two of them laughed in my face, and the other one hung up the phone on me. One of them, Norman Amster, said, "well, why don't you come over and we'll give you a couple of games and see what happens?" That has always been my way to get an opportunity and make the most of it.

So, I took that bus over to St. Petersburg and worked a couple of games. The next year, I was not only umpiring the Mets fantasy camp, but I was also supplying umpires for that camp and four other camps. That was a nice gig. It was because I was umpiring the Mets fantasy camp. One of the Mets front office people, a wonderful man named Arthur Richman, who at the time was the traveling secretary and was in charge of getting umpires for the intrasquads and the games that weren't on the schedule that Major League Baseball and Minor League Baseball does not provide umpires for.

Perry with Arthur Richman

There's lots of those games going on during spring training for all of the clubs. I was just lucky enough to be there on the field in St. Pete doing a fantasy camp. Mr. Richman saw me umpiring and, bless his heart, didn't think, "well, that's weird. That's a woman." Instead, he walked over to me, and said, "Dolly, I need umpires for spring training games. Would you like to umpire?"

I thought about it for about five seconds, and I said, "that is the best proposal I ever got. I do!" So, I took it, and I have run with that one, too. Through that nice sinecure that I acquired through Mr. Richman's auspices, I am

still umpiring Mets spring training games every year. I've umpired
most of the teams in the Grapefruit League: The Red Sox, Phillies,
Blue Jays, Reds.

Perry works the plate at Mets spring training

I'm making my way over to Arizona, slowly but surely. I'm
trying to break in. Do some spring training games over there. Working major league spring training has given me a lot of caché in my
other umpiring pursuits, which are mostly in amateur ball, which
is high school, college, youth leagues, senior men's, men's leagues.
And the last six years, a lot of women's leagues also, because as
I grow older, I'm getting more into the women who are playing.

Understanding that they are still facing the same struggles that
I faced when I started out as an umpire. So, I want to do everything
I can to help bring women's baseball and set up an infrastructure for women players and umpires. So, that women are naturally
drawn into the pipelines that lead to positions as players in leagues
all around the country. And for umpires to get into the pipeline
leading to jobs as professional umpires: high school, college, and
high-level amateur baseball. International baseball.

There are so many leagues. So much baseball all over the world.
Not just here in the United States, but all over Europe and even
in the Middle East. In Pakistan and India. They have leagues and
programs to draw women umpires and players, whereas here in
the United States, we're really in the infancy of getting that going.

You're an advisor for Baseball for All, which creates opportunities for girls and women to play, coach, and umpire at any level. How's that going?

Justine Siegal has been working to get an organization going for girls and women who play baseball since she was a teenager. We're setting up an infrastructure, getting a clearinghouse going, instilling in girls who play baseball and spreading the message to other girls that this is something that is fun. It's rewarding. There is a future after Little League baseball for girls contrary to what a lot of people believe. There is the USA National Women's Team, which is going to be playing up in Canada. A big international tournament coming up soon and the Americans routinely do very well.

Perry counsels a player at a Baseball For All tournament.

In spite of the fact that other countries have these great programs that they get women into and they train them hard. Japan and the Asian countries, wow, those players are really good. Tough competition. And the USA women hold their own against them in spite of the fact that they don't play together a lot. Most of the time when they play as a team, it's just before the event that they are playing in.

They don't get a lot of practice time together, which makes it a lot harder and yet they still manage to hold their own and do well in these international competitions. So, Justine is making it possible for all of us, including me as an umpire, to be together with other women because it's a very lonely feeling being out there and thinking that I'm the only one.

For a long time as an umpire, I felt that I was alone. I had very, very few other women that I ever got a chance to umpire with. My twin sister umpired for six years. But then, she had children and had a regular life. And I kept umpiring. I wondered why other women didn't see me umpiring and ask, "how did you get started? What can I do?"

Justine has made it possible for me to start spreading that message. To get the word out to other women that this is something, that women bring something special to the table when it comes to umpiring. I didn't understand this until I started working with Justine and holding clinics for her ballplayers.

When I do drills for what we call "whackers" at first base, there is a difference between the way the girls respond to the training and make their calls and the way men, grown men, do it at umpire school. I went six times, which is many more times than most umpires go.

So, I have a pretty good handle on the level of competence and the graduating skill level as one goes through the five-week training. Girls on those whackers at first base, most of them are right on those calls. At umpire school, I'd say about 60 percent of the students get those calls correct. The girls, 95 percent. It's mind-boggling. And I'm not saying that we're more accurate or that we see better.

But it's just something that girls and women bring; a focus; a level of dedication. Maybe it's because we feel like we're starting out with a strike against us and that we have to prove ourselves. We have to prove ourselves that we're better than the men and deserve to be judged on an equal footing with them. So, we work very hard, and we are open and receptive to information. We don't take criticism and go cry in a corner because somebody said, "well, you didn't make that call the right way."

Women are just great. Every woman that I've umpired with in my life, and I probably umpired with about thirty or forty now at this point; they are all good. And I can't say that about all the men I've worked with, which obviously there's a greater number and thousands probably. But there are a lot that just really shouldn't be out there in spite of the fact that they are. I don't understand how they can't objectively see that they should direct their energies towards doing something else because they don't have the skills or the people skills either, which are very important in umpiring.

Why are American women still struggling to play baseball in their own country?

Baseball traditionally is very slow to change. It has always had to be dragged, kicking and screaming into the next decade, the next century. It took a long time for black players to become integrated, even after Jackie Robinson vaulted over the color line. It wasn't broken until every team had a black ballplayer and it didn't happen for another twelve years when the Boston Red Sox, finally in 1959, signed "Pumpsie" Green.

So, that's baseball's habit to be very slow in social awareness. That's the pattern for women. We have not been welcomed, but we are starting to be recognized for our skills because of the efforts of people like Justine, as well as the women of the All-American Girls Professional Baseball League who played back in the forties and the fifties and proved to everybody that women and girls can play baseball.

Then somehow, we were forgotten for the next forty years while other girls were still playing high school baseball. Filing lawsuits to play Little League baseball. Just little pockets of girls here and there. But now, we feel like we have a community of girls and women for the first time that did not exist even as recently as 10–15 years ago. So, I think things are about to start changing very rapidly, and it's not going be as difficult a proposition for the girls that are coming along now that are starting out at 6–7–8-years-old; for them to continue and to see that there is a future. So they don't have to give up baseball and become softball players when they go to high school. That baseball is a possibility in their lives and that they continue to play it, be successful, travel and inspire other girls and women to play and umpire.

What does that ball feel like when you hold it in your hands?

Five to five and a quarter ounces. Nine inches in circumference. It can vary a little bit. This is where all the hopes and dreams of every little girl and boy that ever dreamed of being a major league baseball player rests. And there's just something so special about a baseball.

There's nothing like it that's so precious and so beautiful. And it doesn't have to be clean to be beautiful either. It can be all scuffed up and used. And it's just as beautiful.

It's designed to be held and thrown. There's just magic in the baseball. As an umpire, I don't handle the baseball very much, but I see it. I see it in a very specific and special way that very few other people get to see a baseball coming right at me. All there is between me and the baseball is hopefully a decent catcher.

Girls are good catchers. They smother. They're all over everything. They are not afraid of the baseball. Some catchers are afraid of the baseball. They'll turn where they're not protected. They'll turn their heads. I tell 'em, "your protection is in front of you. Don't shift." The girls that play, they are just fearless. And it's just so wonderful to see that. Baseball is a way to express my love for life. It's a gift to me that I try to give back to other people. It's the gift that keeps on giving. And it's just a beautiful way to get people together in a spirit of teamwork and camaraderie and friendship. Even though teams are competing against each other, the best baseball is always when the competitors meet at the end and shake hands no matter who wins or who loses.

My attitude is always that you can learn as much from losing, sometimes, even more than you can from winning. Baseball is not all about success because even the most successful hitters fail seven out of ten times. Those lessons are what baseball is all about. It's doing your best and not dwelling on the mistakes that you made and keeping moving forward and embracing all of the lessons and the wonderful things that baseball has to offer, which are never-ending and boundless.

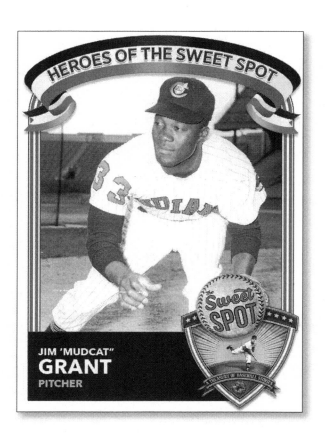

HEROES OF THE SWEET SPOT

JIM 'MUDCAT"
GRANT
PITCHER

JIM "MUDCAT" GRANT

"There were some white catchers that would tell the hitter what was coming because they didn't want you to do well as a black pitcher."

Quick. Name the first African-American to notch twenty wins in the American League. He also was the first black pitcher to start a World Series game for the American League. Meet James Timothy "Mudcat" Grant, pitcher. A visit with "Mudcat" is like a visit with baseball history. From 1958–1971, Mud played for the Indians, Twins, Cardinals, Expos, Dodgers, Pirates, and A's. His roommate was Larry Doby. His teammate was Roberto Clemente. Finding success as both a starter and a relief pitcher from the 1950s to the 1970s, "Mudcat" persevered in the face of racism to blaze a trail of glory on and off the diamond.

MY MOM WAS SOMETHING SPECIAL. She taught me to sing. In fact, she wanted to make sure that I knew the Gospel. It has to do with religion; it has to do with baptism. I was baptized in a river where there were a lot of alligators. What they used to do, the church had these sticks that they would hit the water and chase the alligators away before we were baptized, but she wanted that special baptism.

She always taught me to not be like them. When I say, "Not be like them," these were segregationists, these were the Ku Klux Klan, these were people who didn't particularly care for black folk.

She taught me; she said, "There's one thing that you got to understand: I don't ever want you to be like that. I want you to understand what love is all about."

Mudcat's mother, Viola Grant
(Courtesy of Mudcat Grant)

She taught me very strongly to look out for the hungry, to look out for the not-so-good person and to try to change them, make life a little bit better for them, in terms of conversation, in terms of food, and so forth. She was a strong influence on me.

Faith played a big role, because being taught faith, being taught the understanding of harmony was very important to me. That's the way that I was taught, and that's the way that I was so far all of my life. I'm an old-fashioned Baptist.

How did you first come to baseball?

I became the batboy for the Lacoochee Nine Devils. It was a lumber mill team, and my uncle played on that team.

The Lacoochee Nine Devils taught me every position. I had to learn to catch, I had to learn to pitch, everything. I really didn't know after a period of about six years how good I was. I didn't know that I was a good hitter. I was a good fielder, only because those lumber mill guys taught me the game of baseball. That's how I became part of the baseball folklore with the Lacoochee Nine Devils.

You grew up in the Jim Crow South and faced racism and discrimination throughout your career. How did your attitude about the injustices African-Americans faced evolve from the '50s through the '60s and the '70s?

You come in one, two, three, four, five different thought patterns, because first, you have to look out for your life when it comes to discrimination, when it comes to that kind of anger, when it comes to a circumstantial situation where, if you were born in the South, no matter where you were, you were subject to violence, especially if you stayed in one section of your hometown and another section, of course, always was against you and actually had the rights to do harm to you.

Lacoochee, a lumber mill town, in 1939,
four years after Mudcat was born.
(Courtesy Florida State Archives)

We had to run like hell in many circumstances. I remember when the Ku Klux Klan used to ride through our hometown, and they would shoot into your home. My mom would put us in a wood box for protection until the Ku Klux Klan would run through our hometown. Then, we would come out of the wood box.

There was fear, all right, but also there was substantial thought in terms of survival, because she worked so hard to keep us from being harmed.

What was your first big league spring training camp experience like?

Indians outfielder and Hall of Famer, Larry Doby
(Courtesy Cleveland Public Library)

My first roommate was Larry Doby, who was the first African-American player in the American League. When I went to spring training with the Cleveland Indians big ball club, because I had spent four years in the minor leagues, they told me that I was rooming with Larry Doby. Larry Doby was my hero from a ten-year-old kid.

I said, "I am not rooming with Larry Doby."

They said, "Yes, you are. You are rooming with Larry Doby."

So, what happened was that they put me in the room, and Larry Doby was in the camp. When he came back to the room and I heard that door open, I stood up, and Larry Doby says, "You must be Mudcat Grant."

I said, "Yes, sir, Mr. Doby."

He says, "Well, you're rooming with me. Which bed do you want? This bed?"

I said, "Yes, sir, Mr. Doby."

He said, "You like television?"

I said, "Yes, sir, Mr. Doby."

He said, "Now, listen: We've got to stop this 'Yes, sir, Mr. Doby.'"

I said, "Yes, sir, Mr. Doby."

Anyway, he started teaching me about the difficulties that I was going to face. Even though I had spent four years in the minor leagues, Fargo, North Dakota was a great city for a young black ballplayer, because they treated us with respect. There was no discrimination!

I enjoyed that aspect of it, but Larry taught me what was to come, because I thought that once I got to the major leagues, there would be no more discrimination, but that was not true, because going to Baltimore, we couldn't stay in the same hotel [with the rest of the team] my first year in the big leagues. I learned from Larry about discrimination in terms of the big leagues, even though I knew in the minor leagues what was going to happen. I learned pretty quickly that the difficulties of racism exist no matter where you are.

You were friends with Dr. Martin Luther King.

Martin was a great man. There's no doubt about it. Him being a Southerner and me being a Southerner, that part existed from a vulnerable standpoint, and you had to understand the strength that you needed, the strength that you had in terms of the Lord above, the strength you were going to develop to keep in your mind that, like my mother said, "You can't act like them," per se, "You can't be like them.".

You needed this religious strength to, no matter how badly you were treated, you were not to treat another human being the same way. Martin was adamant on that, and I learned so much just from his philosophy.

What was one of the first major racial issues you faced in pro baseball?

In 1957, I was in the Pacific Coast League. That was when I met my wife-to-be.

Somebody took her to a baseball game, and we were introduced. I was playing for the

Jim "Mudcat" Grant — San Diego Padres

(Photo and card courtesy Doug McWilliams)

San Diego Padres at the time, and the Coast League existed with some great ballplayers, Steve Bilko and all of those guys. She wanted to go to a baseball game, and it just so happened that I met her. In fact, I met her in a lounge which had great musicians, had great blues players, like Earl Grant and O.C. Smith. Then [former Brooklyn Dodger pitcher] Joe Black, the great Joe Black, I met her again through Mr. Black. It sort of evolved to the point now we are dating.

There was a rumor among us black ballplayers that you weren't going to get married to a white person, a white lady.

I was called into the front office of the Cleveland Indians, and they said, "We understand that you are dating this white lady."

I said, "Yes, I am."

They said, "Well, that don't happen in the big leagues." That was the name of that tune.

◆◆◆

Mudcat wanted to marry this "white lady," Trudy, who was his girlfriend, but she feared it would end his career. They would go their separate ways and marry other people. Mudcat ended up getting divorced, and Trudy's husband passed away. They got back together and were finally married in 1984. They remain a devoted couple to this day.

**Mudcat with wife Trudy
(Courtesy Mudcat Grant)**

You were involved in a racial incident before a game in 1960. What happened?

We were playing the Yankees, and I remember because there were about 40-45,000 people in the ballpark at that time at Cleveland Stadium.

When they played the National Anthem, I said, "And this land is not so free, 'cause I can't go to Birmingham, sit down at the coun-tee."

[Indians pitching coach Ted Wilks] Mr. Wilks, he didn't like that, and he said, "Well, if you don't like our country, why the hell won't you get out of our country?"

I said, "If I wanted to leave the country, all I'd have to do is go to Texas [Mudcat knew Wilks was from Texas], and Texas is worse than Russia," or something like that.

[Wilks responded, "if we catch your nigger ass in Texas, we're going to hang you from the nearest tree."][1]

When he said that, we both got into it. Fists were thrown, and so forth and so on.

Indians pitching coach Ted Wilks, 1960
(Courtesy Cleveland Indians)

I was suspended for the rest of the season. I think my suspension was lifted, all right, but I was suspended for making derogatory statements about the National Anthem.

Was there was another incident in 1962 during a game in Kansas City?

Yes. They asked me to pinch-run. That would have been the winning run because we were playing a doubleheader that day. I went out to

---

1   *Jim "Mudcat" Grant, The Black Aces, p. 219, Aventine Press*

first base to pinch run, because if you could run, even though you were a pitcher, and they asked you to pinch run, that's what you did. I went out to first base to pinch run, and [first base coach] Ray Katt, he told me, "If this guy hits a 'tweener [a batted ball that splits the fielders], I want you to act like you've got two watermelons and a man's after you with a shotgun." Then I said to myself, "Did he really say that to me?" I said, "I think he did!"

Indians coach Ray Katt, 1962
(Courtesy Cleveland Indians)

[Mudcat walked off the field in disgust]. He realized that he had made a mistake by telling me that, so he said, "Come back, come back." I took my time, and I walked across the infield.

The fans, the people, they didn't know what I was doing, but I walked in the dugout.

It wasn't [manager] Jimmy Dykes, but somebody told me, "Get back out there!"

In Kansas City at that time, the clubhouse was way up, so I took my time, and I walked back up into that clubhouse, and I didn't go back out there.

Willie Kirkland, who was an outfielder, he sort of made fun of it to take away some of the sting of the whole thing. Now, Willie Kirkland is an African-American.

Willie Kirkland was on the Indians with Mudcat from 1961–1963. (Courtesy Cleveland Indians)

He came out of the shower because I hadn't showered yet, and he looked at me, and he said, "Hey, Mudcat!"

I said, "What?"

He looked at me, and he did this [holding up imaginary

watermelons under each arm]. It was so tense in that clubhouse, but when he did that, it broke up the clubhouse, it broke up the tension.

I suffered for the rest of the season, and I say, "suffered," from a jokingly standpoint. They would always look at me, and they would go like this [holding watermelons under each arm] with these two watermelons. Oh, boy.

How did you meet John F. Kennedy in 1961?

We were in Detroit playing the Tigers, and I got this phone call.

Usually, you didn't get phone calls [in your hotel room] in those days, because you got threatening calls all the time, "So-and-so, you'd better not show up."

Not only me but [Don] Newcombe, Jackie Robinson. Everybody got crazy phone calls that, "if you show up, you're going to be shot, and so forth and so on," so we didn't answer the telephone.

There was a knock on the door. I said, "Who is it?"

They say, "Mudcat, the president had us call you."

I said, "President?"

"Really," they said, "the president, President Kennedy, would like to have breakfast with you."

So I opened the door, and it was the president's Secret Service. They took me to the president.

He said to me; "Mudcat, I really hate to bother you."

I said, "Mr. President, you're not bothering me. I would love to have breakfast with you!"

So, I had breakfast with the president, and we became friends. I was invited to the White House later that summer. During the breakfast conversation with President Kennedy, he asked me a ton of questions. He was well aware of racist circumstances back in those days.

Bobby [Kennedy] was there also.

He said, "Well, where is this hometown you live at, Lacawoochee?"

I said, "It's Lacoochee!"

He said, "Oh! [laughs] Okay. Tell me about Lacoochee."

I said, "Well, Lacoochee is a segregated town. It's a lumber mill town, and the school is segregated."

He said, "Really?"

I said, "Yes, sir. The school is segregated."

I said, "We really don't have enough equipment. We don't have enough books. We don't have enough pencils. The pencils that we have is about that long." [holds fingers a couple of inches apart]

President John F. Kennedy and Mudcat Grant,
circa 1961 (Photo courtesy Mudcat Grant)

He said, "Tell me more about this school." And I did.

Then he said, "You know, I think we're going to make some changes in the South, and your school will be able to get books, be able to get crayons, be able to get as educated as anybody else."

I said, "Mr. President, can you do that?"

He said, "I *think* I can," and he sure did.

He changed the housing. He changed the education system to the point where education was free, and it was a way of having the same kind of education that everybody else, all of the whites, were getting at this time. It was President Kennedy that did that.

When I told my mom that I had met the president, "Well, boy, you didn't meet the president."

I said, "Mom, I met the president." I said, "We are going to be able to get pencils. We're going to be able to get books. We're going to be as educated as anybody else," but what was funny about that was that the education that we did have was outstanding.

Those black teachers in Lacoochee, Florida at that school, whatever kind of books we had or whatever kind of pencils, no matter how short they were, it was unbelievable how they taught us! We graduated on time.

Willie Mays was criticized during his playing days for not being more outspoken about racism and being a part of the Civil Rights Movement. Is that fair?

It really wasn't fair, because you could've said that about any African-American athlete at that time because there was a way that African-American athletes did their thing. A lot of times, it was the way Willie Mays did it, by simply being Willie Mays. A lot of times, it was a little bit different way. Maybe another athlete treated it a little bit more doing less, but actually silently doing more.

Yeah, it's unfair that Willie Mays was portrayed that way because as far as I was concerned, he did a great job of making sure that we were as good as anybody else. He didn't have to do any more than he did because when I see Willie now, I look at him and I see not only a great ballplayer, but the harmony of his life, of his way of doing things, I thought was great.

Did you have many conversations with Jackie Robinson along the way?

I sure did. I met Jackie during the Larry Doby days, when he became a broadcaster. I met him again when I was with the Minnesota Twins.

He said, "What are you going to do after you get out of baseball?"

I said, "I am going to become a singer."

He said, "You're going to become a singer?"

I said, "Yeah, that's what I want my career to be after I get out of the game of baseball."

"No, you need to do more than that." He said, "Did you finish college?"

I said, "No, I only have two years of college."

He said, "I think you need to finish your college career, and I think you need to work on patterns a little bit stronger than being a singer in life."

We had conversations like that several times after that. He thought there should be a stronger effort in terms of what you were going to do with your life after baseball.

In your Black Aces book, you state that Cincinnati Reds manager Birdie Tebbetts denied one of his pitchers, Brooks Lawrence, the chance to win 20 games in 1956 because he did not want a black 20-game winner on his watch. Tebbetts was also your manager in 1963 and part of 1964. Was he an overt racist?

Frank "Pinky" Higgins managed the Boston Red Sox from 1955–1962. (Courtesy of the Boston Public Library, Leslie Jones Collection)

Birdie Tebbetts wasn't the only one. There was [Boston Red Sox manager] Pinky Higgins, who told Earl Wilson he was never going to be a 20-game winner as long as he was the manager. Those were routine circumstances back in them days. Of course, Earl Wilson was traded to the Detroit Tigers after that, but, there was something about becoming a 20-game winner if you were a black man that was kind of strange about the whole thing, but we sort of got used to comments like that, because if it would've shocked somebody else to hear that comment, it didn't shock us.

It didn't shock African-Americans because those were the thought patterns, that was the way it was back in those days. It didn't mean anything to me because those comments we've heard plenty of times. "You're not going to become a 20-game winner," because they had this thing about a black pitcher winning 20 games.

Pitcher Earl Wilson and infielder Elijah "Pumpsie" Green (Courtesy of the Boston Public Library, Leslie Jones Collection)

It's kind of hard to figure out where they were coming from. To me, as long as you took your turn to go out there to pitch, if it would've been 50 games, who cares, as long as you were winning games to help your team? It was very odd back in them days, but that's what happened.

Not only managers, but catchers [conspired against black pitchers]. Your catcher that you were throwing the ball to didn't necessarily want you to do well, either. It's like the black quarterback; they just didn't think that we were smart enough, or if they thought we were smart enough to become 20-game winners, for some reason, to them, it was something against them.

You sort of wondered why, but you didn't really have to wonder why a long time because the thought patterns of that particular thing was there. I won't call their names, but there were some catchers that you crossed them up deliberately to get their attention so that you could get a hitter out. There were some catchers that would tell the hitters, the opposing player, what was coming because they didn't want you to do well as a pitcher back in those days. To us, you had to go beyond that circumstance and win the ballgame anyway, but now you're not only pitching against the opposing team; you're pitching against your own catcher.

If all of those 20-game winners from *The Black Aces* book were in this room today, they would admit that they had difficulties with white catchers who didn't want black pitchers to become 20-game winners.

You were traded from Cleveland to Minnesota on June 15th, 1964. The Minnesota Twins at that time were owned by Calvin Griffith, a prejudiced individual. What were your thoughts on playing for such a man?

You see, having to play for such a man, in terms of your thoughts, made you much more compettive. I shouldn't say "much more," but it made you more competitive, because of the stance of a guy like Calvin Griffith had back in those days. It is like a Jackie Robinson thought. It's like a Larry Doby thought, like a Luke Easter thought.

Larry Doby told me, "Let me tell you something: You're going to face a lot of problems. You're going to face a lot of problems that is racist, but when you go out there on that mound," he said, "you go out there to win, regardless of what anybody thinks, regardless of what they may say. When you get out on that mound, and you're facing Ted Williams, whoever you're facing, you're out there to win ballgames, and you keep that in mind."

By the time I got to Minnesota, and by the time we all, African-Americans and black Cubans too, black Puerto Ricans, we knew that this man [Griffith] had some difficulties in terms of what he thought. That didn't stop us from trying to win ballgames. That was the strength of African-Americans and Afro-Cubans back then. That's the way we thought.

Indians outfielder, roommate, and good friend
Larry Doby (Courtesy Cleveland Indians)

I heard you have two nicknames. One was given to you as a child, and one when you were an adult. The first was "Black Jesus."

Yeah, they used to call me "Black Jesus" because I never got in trouble as a kid. My mama had a lot to do with that, you see, because if you had a mom like mine and you got in trouble, you were in some *serious* trouble, I'll tell you that. Because I never got in trouble, because I never missed a day of school, never missed a Sunday of church, never got in trouble with my fellow kids and so they used to call me "Black Jesus."

Mudcat on the Twins
(Courtesy Minnesota Twins)

If some other person or kid suggested that, "Well, you know, that James Grant said he did this and he did that," the rest of the kids said, "Uh-uh. Uh-uh. That's Black Jesus! He never been in no trouble. He ain't gon' get in no trouble because of that woman over there," talking about my mom.

So, yeah, my nickname was "Black Jesus" because I didn't get in any kind of trouble. I was always helpful to the other kids. The reason I have golf tournaments and the reason I make appearances when it comes to food is because of my mom. That was just the way she was. She used to make me go fishing. She would cook the fish, she would make sandwiches, and then what we would do, me, my brother, and my sister, is that we would take food to the hungry.

Not only did we take food to the hungry, but also you had to give the food to the head of the household. The head of the household, then, would disperse the food the way that it should be dispersed.

That's what I learned. That's what I was taught. If Mrs. Kate needed her wood cut, she needed a wood pile from the lumber mill; I had to make sure that we cut enough wood for her to use in a stove to do the cooking.

In Lacoochee, Florida, we have a Boys', Girls' Club that I helped put together. We have a benefit golf tournament, we have Food for Thought, and we have Wounded Warriors. We have several charities. We visit hospitals.

Our celebrities, what we do is, we go to those hospitals and we spend time with the patients there. That's easy for me, and it's easy for my celebrities that go to do these functions. Up at Syracuse, we have a diabetic golf tournament, also. It's easy because that's the way I was taught.

The other nickname is the one you carry to this day. How did that come about?

In the minor leagues, in the minor league camp, we had about maybe 450 to 500 minor league ballplayers back in the day. If you were black, you thought all black ballplayers was from Mississippi. That's the way they thought back in those days, so they just started calling me "Mississippi Mudcat," because they thought I was from Mississippi.

Then they dropped the Mississippi, and they started calling me "Mudcat," and the name stuck. There was a news article, and somebody passed it to my mom.

They said, "Did you see this news clipping?" and it said, "there's a kid in camp for the Cleveland Indians who has a chance, maybe, to become a big leaguer one day, and his name is Mudcat Grant."

Somebody says, "Is that your son?"

She said, "That's not. I don't have no son named 'Mudcat Grant.'"

We didn't have telephones back in those days. So, my mom wrote me a letter that says, "Is that you?"

I said, "Yes."

Mom was the best of everything. In fact, in the '65 World Series, [Mudcat and his Minnesota Twins faced the Los Angeles Dodgers, losing in seven games] Mom was sitting in a section where they had some Dodger fans, and what happened is that this Dodger fan, he started on me right away.

He said, "We're going to knock that bum out of there. We're going to knock that bum out."

Mom was sitting there, and even though Mom wasn't a baseball fan, she noticed that "We're going to knock that bum out."

So, Mom said, "Are you talking about that man out there?"

He said, "Yeah. We're going to knock that bum out."

So my mom said, "That's my son, and he ain't no bum."

They didn't pay too much attention, "We're going to knock that bum out!"

So, my mom took her pocketbook and hit him at the back of his head.

He said, "Oh no, no, Lord!"

She said, "I'm sorry! I'm sorry!"

Oh, boy. That's the way she was. She was spiffy. [laughs heartily]

1965 was your best season as a starter. You won 21 games, leading the American League with six shutouts and fourteen complete games. You started 39 of them. How did all this come together?

It came together that season, 1965, because I met a pitching coach by the name of Johnny Sain, even though my pitching coach at the Cleveland Indians, Mel Harder, was also a great pitching coach. There's no doubt about that. I was sandwiched between two Hall of Famers on that pitching staff over there with the Cleveland Indians: Early Wynn, Hall of Famer, and Bob Lemon, Hall of Famer. I was sandwiched between those, and I learned a lot from them also, but

Johnny Sain had this knack of teaching that he could spot your weakness and he could spot this, he could spot that.

Mudcat was voted to the All-Star team and named The Sporting News American League Pitcher of the Year in 1965.

(Courtesy Minnesota Twins)

He did a great job in putting it all together for me at that time. He taught me a couple of pitches that I could get double plays on.

I was in better shape that year than I was any other time in my career. I was able to finish games. Jim Kaat, who should be in the Hall of Fame and was on that pitching staff also, he won about 19 games that year [Kaat was 18-11 in 1965]. I think Johnny Sain had a lot to do in terms of that outstanding year that I had.

Someone else that might've contributed to your success was a catcher by the name of Earl Battey.

Earl Battey was my catcher, and a great, great person. I'd had problems with catchers before Earl Battey, and he was the first African-American catcher that I spent time with. So the harmony of it all, in terms of that year, Earl Battey had a lot to do with it.

Earl Battey, 3-time gold glove catcher
(Courtesy Minnesota Twins)

He was smart. He was very smart. For the first time, I had a catcher, even though he was African-American, I had a catcher that you could relate to real good that you didn't have this, "You can't do this, you can't do that," [from some of the] white catchers.

With Earl, right away, there was no problem. The harmonious effect that we had with one another in terms of pitching to other hitters and figuring out what to do in terms of the game plan and stuff like that, it was harmonious on that, too. Earl Battey, like Johnny Sain, was responsible for my 20-game season that year. Even though it was one hell of a season, I'll tell you that, it was just unbelievable. Earl Battey, yeah, that's my man.

I had another season, all right, when I became a member of the Oakland A's.

I became a relief pitcher, and I had an outstanding year.[2] [A's catcher] Dave Duncan was like Earl Battey, to tell the truth. He was one hell of a catcher. His thought patterns were harmonious with the kind of pitching that you wanted to do.

What did it mean to you to be the first African-American to win 20 games in the American League?

(Courtesy National Baseball Hall of Fame Library, Cooperstown, NY)

It meant a lot to me. Becoming the first African-American to become a 20-game winner, I think pitching had a lot to do with it that year, but we didn't have a lot of starting black pitchers back at that time in '65. We really didn't in the American League. In the National League, yeah, we had a whole bunch of people over there: the Bob Gibsons, the Don Newcombes, and Joe Blacks.

---

2   *In 1970, Mudcat pitched 80 games for Oakland, and 8 for Pittsburgh, going a combined 9–3 with an earned-run average of 2.03*

That was the time when black pitchers were sort of catching up with continuity of things. The fact that there had not been a black 20-game winner [in the American League] is the reason I say that particular thing. We had a few black pitchers, but not many. Time started catching up now in terms of African-American players and having those records.

The 1965 season culminates with your team, the Twins, getting into the World Series to play the Dodgers.

That World Series in '65, that was something special. When I say "something special," not necessarily overall, but something special in terms of what was about to happen. I was supposed to start that Series against Sandy Koufax. Because of Yom Kippur, Koufax didn't start that game, but I was supposed to start that game. It would've been the first time that a Jewish and an African-American would start a [World Series] game against one another. I wasn't so ready to start against Koufax, knowing the kind of pitcher he was, but on the other hand, I wanted that. We took a picture together before he made the decision not to start that game because of Yom Kippur. That was something special to me.

The photo that I have with him is a wonderful photo. Another great thing that I remember about that is that Koufax and I spent some time in the off-season for Job Corps, young people getting jobs and so forth, so there's another remembrance of that. We had spent some time together for the whole winter, so that was great.

You had some problems with the Twins, stating that some of them were racial because Calvin Griffith wanted you to stop being seen in public with white women. What happened?

I was a little feisty at that time. I think a lot had to do with being feisty at that time is that the off-season and things that happened to me with "Mudcat and His Kittens" [Mudcat's off-season singing group] and other entertainers that were just wonderful. I was not as careful attitude-wise as I ordinarily would have been had I paid a little bit more attention, but now, out singing and meeting other people and them sort of celebrating with you in what you had done in the World Series and so forth, I was not as careful in terms of thought patterns as I ordinarily would have been.

I think that had a lot to do with stretching out a little bit and making more comments. I think before then, whatever Cal Griffith had to say, I wouldn't have even let it bother me one way or another, but I was spouting off a little bit in terms of being, maybe, a little bit more critical of other people.

My mom never said anything to me, but I am sure that there's a couple of times she would've said, "Hey, come here! Come here. Go over there and sit down, and I don't want to hear you talk anymore."

Who were some of the toughest hitters you faced?

The hitters? I'm going to tell you something: Ted Williams is one of the best hitters that I faced. Hank Aaron, one of the best hitters that I've faced. Roberto Clemente, one of the best hitters that I've faced. Mickey Mantle was a pretty good hitter. Rod Carew, I faced briefly, but in watching him, he was one of the best hitters out there. I would say those guys. Ted Williams was a friend. I remember as a rookie starting a game against the Boston Red Sox.

This is [June 23]1958, and Larry Doby said, "You see that guy over there?"

I said, "Yeah." We were at batting practice at this time.

He said, "That's Ted Williams."

I said, "Yeah, I know."

He said, "This is one guy you have to watch out for."

Ted Williams was aware of the fact that this rookie Mudcat Grant was supposed to be pretty good.

Doby and I were at the top of the dugout, and Ted Williams came over and said, "Hi, Larry. How you doing?"

Larry said, "I'm doing pretty good." Ted said, "Is that him?"

Doby said, "Yeah, that's him."

Ted Williams looked at me, and he said, "So, you're pretty good, eh?"

I didn't know what to say at the time. I said, "That's right!"

He said, "Well, I'm going to get a little piece of you today." [laughs]

I said, "Larry, did you hear what he said?"

Larry said, "I heard what he said. He said he's going to get a little piece of you today."

Ted Williams, "The Splendid Splinter," takes batting practice. (Courtesy Boston Public Library, Leslie Jones Collection)

I said, "Well, I'm going to try to get a little piece of *him* today."

Now, nobody ever knocked Ted Williams down. You didn't knock him down.

So, Larry said, "You going to knock him down?"

I said, "I'm going to knock him down."

Now, the game starts. Ted Williams comes up, and I throw one right underneath the chin. He just did that [moves head back slightly], and I went, "Hmm." I moved it over a little bit more, you know, to knock him down. He just did that [moves head slightly].

I said to myself, "I better leave this guy alone. I won't bother Ted Williams anymore." He ended up being a good friend. [Ted went 1-2 with a double off Mudcat that day.[3]]

The Boston Red Sox and the Cleveland Indians played exhibition games after spring training. One of the exhibition places that we played was New Orleans. When you flew into New Orleans, and when you landed, and you came out of the airport, if you were African-American, they didn't want you around at all. We couldn't ride in the bus with the rest of our teammates who were white because they didn't allow blacks and whites to ride together in buses in New Orleans back then. What they would do is take the white players on a bus and we had to go across the street out of the airport, and we had to wait on a black cab to come and pick us up to take us to the hotel.

Well, they would take us to the hotel, but we couldn't check in because they didn't allow African-Americans to stay in the same hotel. They would take us to another black hotel where we would stay. Our bags were with the white players that stayed in New Orleans, and what we had to do, we had to make a pull [a game to determine a winner or loser] to see who was going to go and pick up the bags. That was Earl Wilson, "Pumpsie" Green, me, and Vic Power. They didn't want more than one player to pick up the bags. They thought if there were about two or three black players, that we'd come to steal or something like that. I lose the pull, so I've got to get the bags.

I went to the hotel to get the bags while my teammates went to a black home.

---

3   Dave Heller, *Facing Ted Williams: Players from Baseball's Golden Age Recall the Greatest Hitter that Ever Lived, Sports Publishing*

Soon as I walked up, [the bellman] said, "What are you doing here?"

I said, "Well, I'm one of the African-American players with the Cleveland Indians, and those bags that you see over there, I've got to get."

They said, "You ain't getting no bags from here."

I said, "Well, if you look at those Samsonite bags, they've got our names on them, and those are our bags."

By this time, now, Ted Williams is coming with the trainer. They had spent time going to dinner, and they came back. Soon as Ted saw me, he said, "Hey, Mudcat's here! How you doing?"

I said, "I ain't doing too good." I said, "You know, our bags, and Earl Wilson and "Pumpsie" Green, their bags, I have to pick them up and take them."

He said, "No, you don't have to pick them up and take them. You see that guy right there [points to the bellman]? *He* has to pick them up and take them."

I said, "That's right, boy. Go over there and pick up them bags!" [laughs]

Ted Williams waited. He waited until the guy picked up the bags. He put them in the black cab. The cab driver, he was nervous, man. Where we stayed, at a black home, it took about 45 minutes to get down to the hotel where our bags was, but when they put the bags in the cab, it took that cab about 15 minutes to get back to where we was getting, he was so frightened about the whole episode.

You were both a starter and a reliever, and you're one of only five pitchers to have 20 wins and 20 saves. What's the mindset of both of those types of pitchers?

As a starter, you've got to think in terms of nine innings. I know it's a little bit different ballgame, nowadays. If you get five, six innings, the bullpen takes care of the rest of it. As a starter, that didn't happen back in them days. As a starter, you wanted to pitch nine innings, and you weren't looking for a relief pitcher because to become a 20-game winner, you got to stay in the game as long as you possibly can. If it's a tight game, now, you may not necessarily get a win, and there were no saves back in those days.

They had a system, all right, in terms of bullpen people, but not necessarily a "save" person as a starter back in those days, so you had to think in terms of how long you were going to stay in the ballgame. That's the way it was.

Mudcat pitched for the Montreal Expos in 1969, their first season in MLB.

(Courtesy National Baseball Hall of Fame Library, Cooperstown, NY)

I became a relief pitcher a little bit later, especially with the Oakland A's, and I had the best year that I ever had [1.82 ERA with 24 saves in 72 games], including that season where I won 20 ballgames. As a relief pitcher, that's what you did: you saved games. I became a real good relief pitcher because I could throw strikes and I could throw double play balls and stuff like that. Rollie Fingers gave me a great compliment because I used to sit in the bullpen and Rollie and I used to talk quite a bit. Rollie was a long relief man back in those days.

Hall of Fame reliever Rollie Fingers, 1971
(Photo by Doug McWilliams)

They used to make fun of Rollie, and Rollie and I would talk in the bullpen.

I said, "Rollie, don't let them make fun of you. With the stuff you've got, you can become a real good relief pitcher."

He said, "Really?"

I said, "Yeah."

Every game, we would sit, and we would chat about, "What am I going to do with the stuff that I have?"

When Rollie became a Hall of Famer, he gave me credit for

those days that we spent together talking about becoming a relief pitcher…and I thought that was a wonderful recognition.

What were the pitches in your repertoire?

Mudcat demonstrates throwing with the seam of the ball.

As a starter, I threw with the seam. I threw with the seam, with my thumb underneath the ball. Johnny Sain and I worked on that because you can make the ball move a little bit. If you take it and move it a little bit backwards, the ball is going to move a little bit, but it's not going to move the way that you would take it with the seam. The ball would dip a little bit at the start, at least for me. It would dip just a little bit, and when you're looking for people on base, now you're talking about double plays and so forth. When you released the ball, the ball would move just a little bit this way [downward motion].

If it comes up top and you throw across the seam, that's a little bit different story because the ball now is going to move a little bit this way [slightly to the right] instead of moving that way [to the left]. The hitters are looking at your movement and then looking at your style, but the ball is going to be different every time you throw the ball. This is not to say you're going to get them out [laughs], but it's something that is not the same. The ball moves a little bit different. With people on base, you're looking for the ball to dip or do something so that when the hitters hit the ball, they're hitting the ball with movement on the ball all the time.

Mudcat's grip across the seams

You're talking about movement. You're talking about movement to the left, movement to the right, and it may make a difference, you see what I mean? Obviously, sometimes, it doesn't make no difference.

Mudcat demonstrates his arm movement for a breaking ball.

Instead of looking this way, you're looking that way [arcs head as if watching a ball leave the park] at a home run or something like that. Johnny Sain taught me those things, and we're talking about movement. Movement up, movement down. It's not that simple, but it's pretty much that simple.

Mudcat's breaking ball grip

The breaking ball was mostly this finger [third finger, next to the index finger], mostly with the shoulder-elbow type of movement coming across this way.

It's like a slider, they call it a slider...you could actually throw it inside, where when the hitter wants to really extend, the ball gets onto you much quicker.

What pitches did you learn from Satchel Paige?

Satchel Paige told me, "If you want to become a good pitcher, you've got to throw a titty pitch."

I said, "What is a titty pitch?"

He said, "That pitch right here [holds hand near his chest]. That's a titty pitch."

He said, "To start off a hitter, you've got to pitch inside, what you call a titty pitch. You've got to pitch inside. You've got to make sure that a hitter don't get out there and take everything away. You can back him up a little bit, and you start from there."

That's what Satchel Paige said. "You've got to learn how to throw that pitch at him, no matter who it is." I never forgot that.

Mudcat met Hall of Fame pitcher Satchel Paige in 1955 when they were in the minors together. He credits Paige with teaching him how to pitch.

(Courtesy Negro Leagues Baseball Museum)

Some hitters, it didn't matter what you threw. You could throw a titty pitch; you could throw outside, inside. Yogi Berra, he didn't care about anything. If you threw a titty pitch, if you threw one outside, he hit that, too. That's the way Yogi Berra was. The average hitter has their style of hitting. They like to hit certain pitches and so forth, but Yogi Berra, if you pitched them up there, he'd hit that thing. If you pitched them down here, he'd hit that thing. That's the way Yogi Berra was. He'd hit anything you threw up there at the plate.

Satchel taught you some unique pitches; the Hop and Jumper and the Cloud Ball. What were they?

The Hop and Jumper had something on it. Satchel Paige would put stuff on the ball. I wouldn't call it a spitter, but the Hop and Jumper, if the umpire came out to the mound, if the hitters complained to the umpire that something wasn't right because the ball was doing stuff and the umpire came out, and he would look everywhere, if he didn't see anything, he just says, "Okay, I don't see anything."

Tide [laundry detergent] used to have little slick stuff that you use, and then you just put it on the ball, it would just slip out. That was a Hop and Jumper.

[Ed. note: outfielder Jay Johnstone recalled a story about Mudcat's catcher on the Indians, Joe Azcue, who was going out to the mound and slapping his hands on Mudcat's chest during a game. The umpire wanted to know what was going on. Azcue: "I'm getting him fired up to pitch to the hitter." In reality, the heat of the day generated perspiration, causing the detergent embedded in Mudcat's jersey to produce telltale bubbles, which Azcue was hastily popping before the umpires took notice.]

A Cloud Ball, of course, was like the clouds. It had a little something on it. It was wet, let me put it that way. It was just wet. It was just a name to have fun with, but it was a little damp.

I remember the commissioner said, "What kind of pitch was that?"

I said, "Oh, that was a fastball."

I didn't let the commissioner know I was putting a little stuff on the ball. They were just names for fun.

◆◆◆

You went on a couple of trips to visit US troops in Vietnam with other big leaguers during the war. What was that like?

When we visited Vietnam, there was so many wounded soldiers that they had indoor hospitals. They would bring the soldiers in the helicopters, and they would treat the wounded. If they gave you a Purple Heart on the pillow, that meant you weren't going to live long. Me and several of the ballplayers visited those hospitals.

This one soldier, he had a Purple Heart on, but he wasn't gone yet. He wasn't dead yet, so I went over to his bed. He was unconscious.

I said, "I am Mudcat Grant, and Ron Swoboda is here visiting. I don't know if you can hear me, but if you can hear me, I hope that you make it."

Then I read a couple of poems for him. You move on to another soldier, and you try to do the same thing.

Then, I was with the St. Louis Cardinals [1969], and what happened was that during the season, I got a message saying that, "There's somebody out here that wants to see you."

I went outside, and it was that soldier.

When I went over, and I talked to him, he said, "I had to come because I wanted you to know that I *heard* you."

Talking very faintly in his ear, he did hear me, and he knew that I was Mudcat Grant. He had his wife with him, and I think there was one kid that they had with them. Anyway, we got a chance to shake each other's hand. He said he heard me, so that made me feel pretty good. That made me step pretty good there after that.

> *[Ed. note: Mudcat reports that he continues to see the soldier from time to time at his annual golf tournament in Binghamton, New York.]*

In 1971 you were with the Pittsburgh Pirates during their championship season [Mudcat left the Pirates for the A's August 10, 1971, and did not appear in the World Series]. You appeared in 42 games, pitching 75 innings. That had to be special because

you'd been denied the championship in '65, and now, at the end of your career, you're a world champion.

Mudcat pitched for Pittsburgh in the 1970 and 1971 seasons.

(Courtesy Pittsburgh Pirates)

That meant a lot to me because I was traded to Pittsburgh and Danny Murtaugh was a great guy and one hell of a manager. We used to play pinochle with Danny all day. We used to go to the ballpark at about 10 in the morning, and Danny Murtaugh was a pinochle guy; he loved pinochle, so we would actually get to the ballpark at 9-something in the morning, and we would play until batting practice.

When I first got over there to the Pittsburgh Pirates, Danny Murtaugh asked me, "Are you ready?"

I said, "I'm ready. Anytime you want me to go, I'm ready."

I got in the game as soon as I got over there. We were ahead, 6–4, and they put me in the game. I gave up something like eight runs. I come back to the dugout, and I threw my glove down.

Murtaugh said, "What's the matter?"

I said, "Man, you brought me over here to be a short reliever. I gave up eight runs." This is about the seventh inning.

He said, "Can you hold 'em?"

I said, "I can hold 'em from here."

He said, "Oh, hell, we're going to score about ten or fifteen runs."

We started the next inning, and Vic Davalillo hit a grand-slam home run, and then Willie Stargell hit a two-run homer, and somebody hit a three-run homer. Before you know it, there are all of these runs.

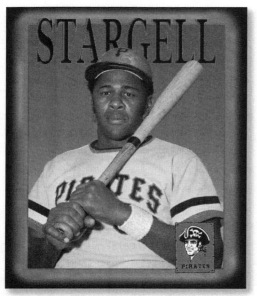

Hall of Famer Willie Stargell was a 2-time world champion, 6-time All-Star, and MVP of the National League in 1979.

(Courtesy Pittsburgh Pirates)

Now, I'm with the Pittsburgh Pirates and all of a sudden, I realize what kind of a ball club they had. They had Manny Sanguillen, Willie Stargell, and Al Oliver.

They were unbelievable and really nice to me. What happened at that time was when you are with a team, and you are with a team during the World Series years, you have to have a team meeting. If you weren't there the whole season, you have to have a team meeting as to who was going to deserve a ring and who was going to get World Series money.

When they made the vote, they didn't vote me for a ring, because I didn't get there until half the season was over or a little bit later, so I didn't think much of it at that time. I just assumed that that was it. Now, I'm at a dinner in New York, and Willie Stargell is at that dinner. Willie had his wife with him.

Stargell said, "Mudcat."

I said, "What?"

He said, "Where's your ring?"

I said, "I didn't get voted a ring. Didn't you know that?"

He said, "No, man." He said, "You're going to get a ring."

I said, "Am I going to get a World Series ring?"

He said, "You were on that team. This is what you did," and so forth and so on. Time passed. There was an affidavit that was signed. Willie Stargell got all of the ballplayers to make that signature, so I did get the ring.

Dock Ellis was on that Pirates team with you and called himself "the first militant of baseball." You were a little bit older than Dock. What kind of a guy and a teammate was he?

Dock was different. When I got to Pittsburgh, they told me that I was rooming with Dock. He was a great guy. He left way too early, way too early. [Ellis died 2008/12/19 at age 63].

Dock looked at me and said, "So, you're the Mudcat?"

I said, "Yep. I'm the Mudcat."

He said, "I heard about you."

That was the beginning of it. I used to do flips with cards and stuff like that. Flips with cards was, you take your cap, and you put your cap down, and then you take a deck of cards, and you flip them in the cap. Then you take two decks of cards, and you take two cards and you flip them in the cap.

Dock, he kept watching me. I would flip, and sometimes, I would take three cards, and I would flip three cards in a cap.

Dock, finally, he said, "What are you doing?" I said, "I'm practicing my control.

He said, "Really?"

I said, "Yeah. The weight of the cards is what I am looking for, because if you play flips with the cards, if you take one card, and if you flip and the card goes in…you know where your control is. If you take two cards, and you flip, if you notice, you don't flip as high as the card."

Dock said, "Really?"

I said, "Yeah."

I took three cards and I flipped three cards. The next night, I saw Dock flipping cards. He was just flipping cards. He wanted to know the weight of the cards.

I said, "Now take them and turn it over and you've got a slider." I told him, "You've got a slider. If you slide with this finger and that finger, that's like flipping two cards. It's just turning it over the other way."

He did, and that's what he would do.

Now, I got to spring training, and I believed, physically, that you had to get in shape. I would go to the ballpark early, and I would do my running and get in shape. Then Dock ended up doing the same thing, running and getting in shape.

He was different, and he threw a no-hitter on LSD, but he was okay. Dock Ellis was really okay. He was a good man, and he loved the game of baseball. He was different.

I wish he could've stayed around a little bit longer. We would've seen some different stuff about Dock Ellis. He was a good man.

Talk about some of your teammates. Start with your first club, the Cleveland Indians, and pitcher Gary Bell.

I took Gary Bell up to Harlem because he wanted to see James Brown, Gladys Knight and the Pips, and The Temptations. I took Gary, Woodie Held, and Sam McDowell to the Apollo Theater in Harlem. We were in town playing the Yankees, and I called up the

Apollo Theater, and I said, "I have some guys that I want to bring to the theater. Could you get me some tickets?"

They said, "Of course." The game went a little bit too long, but after the game, I took them to the Apollo Theater.

The show had already started. When we all got in the theater, the lights were down, so nobody saw these three white guys coming in the theater. The show is over, and the lights come up, and there was all of these black folk and just these three white guys, so I ran off and left them. I ran off and left Gary Bell, Woodie Held, Sam McDowell with all of these black folk, and they ran me down. [laughs] That was a lot of fun.

Gary was also your roommate, wasn't he?

Yeah. Baseball didn't want black and white roommates, but in the American League, Gary Bell and I were the first. Now, in terms of roommates, the fact that they didn't want black and white roommates, but if you wanted to room together, they made you pay for your room. That was the way it was.

Gary Bell was a 3-time All-Star pitcher and Mudcat's roommate on the Indians.

(Courtesy Cleveland Indians)

Gary and I decided that we were going to room together. He was my friend; I was his friend. We paid for the room, and we were the first black and white roommates in the American League. Gary Bell not only was my roommate, but he was a friend of mine, and his mom loved me. Gary's mom loved me. We're still friends to this day.

How about Leon "Daddy Wags" Wagner, slugger and outfielder with the Indians?

Leon Wagner was a 2-time All-Star and one of the game's great characters. (Courtesy Cleveland Indians)

Leon was a different guy. He was funny, also. We had a curfew one night. When you have a curfew, that means you're supposed to be in bed two hours after the game. They had a checker. They had one of the coaches that would check to make sure that the players were in bed. We had this doubleheader, and we're supposed to be in bed, and Wagner decided that he was going to go out.

Wagner was my roomie, and I said, "Wagner, you can't. You can't go."

He said, "Oh, I'm going. I'm going. I'm not going to stay here. I've got a couple of places to go."

The guy comes and he checked the bed.

He said, "You guys in?"

I said, "Everybody in."

Now, Wagner got dressed. We're in the Chicago American Hotel. They've got long corridors. Now he leaves out of the room and he goes down this long corridor, and one of the coaches come around the corner. While Wagner is coming down, he stretched out his hands like he's sleepwalking.

When he passed the coach, he said, "By the way, when you wake up, that's a $100 fine."

Wagner, he was a character. He was a good hitter. Couldn't field that well, but he was a character.

What are your reflections of Roberto Clemente?

Hall of Famer Roberto Clemente won the NL MVP in 1966, four batting titles, and twelve gold gloves. Mudcat and Clemente were teammates in 1970 and 1971 with Pittsburgh. Clemente died in a plane crash 1972/12/31 while attempting to deliver supplies to earthquake victims in Nicaragua.

(Courtesy Pittsburgh Pirates)

Roberto Clemente was one of the best ballplayers that I played with, and he was one of the best I played against. Good man. That was a very sad day. Roberto wanted to take some goods, relief, to the people that were affected by the earthquake.

Man, it was a bad time. It was unfortunate. Not only did they find none of the stuff, they didn't find Roberto. They didn't find anybody.

What would've been even more tragic is the fact that [Pirates catcher Manny] Sanguillen was supposed to go with Roberto Clemente, but he was late. He drove up, but by the time he drove up, the plane was taking off. Otherwise, Sanguillen would've been gone too. Roberto was a good guy. He was a nice man. Of the ballplayers that I played with and played against, he's one of the best. There's no doubt about that.

What kind of shape was your body in when you hung 'em up?

I was in good shape when I retired because when I retired, I didn't get hired after my last season of employment in the major leagues. There was nothing wrong with my body, there was nothing wrong with my arm, but there was something wrong with my salary. What I was making, they didn't want to pay. It just so happened that I didn't get a contract, but there was nothing wrong with my arm. If you check, I had as many saves then as when I first became a relief pitcher, see, so I was still pitching well.

I used to wonder sometime; I said, "Did somebody think something about me or something?"

But I didn't get another contract. I did have problems with Joe Brown, the general manager for the Pittsburgh Pirates, but I don't know exactly why I didn't get another contract. That was it. I did go to the minor leagues. I did that, and I was the pitching coach for the Oakland A's minor league team. Other than that, I didn't get back to the major leagues again, even though I was productive.

◆◆◆

Music has played a big role in your life. Talk about how Mudcat and the Kittens came to be.

Mudcat and the Kittens! Boy, I tell you, the Kittens were great. When I decided to do music, I wanted to do music in a way where I would make sure that I could get hired as a musician, as a singer, but also I wanted something a little bit different, so I came up with "Mudcat and His Kittens."

A publicity photo from Mudcat's days as a singer and entertainer (Courtesy Mudcat Grant)

There were six of them in the beginning, and then it went to four, then to five, then it went back to six. I had one hell of a time with my girls. They could sing, they could dance. They were great girls, all of them. It turned out to be a real good show. I enjoyed it very much.

You've got a baseball in your hands. When you hold that baseball, what does your heart and soul say?

When I hold this ball, this ball tells the story of a young kid that was lucky enough to be the batboy of the Lacoochee Nine Devils, was lucky enough to travel this country and other countries, was lucky enough to be in some situations where you got a chance to fight for equality, got a chance to develop a friendship of players of all kinds, got a chance to meet people like Billie Holiday and Nat Cole, The Supremes, The Temptations, got a chance to actually be a part of life that a kid from Lacoochee could possibly think of, and got a chance to do some other things that had to do with society, had a chance to change the minds of some people.

I remember [Twins teammate and pitcher from North Carolina] Jim Perry at one time could've been racist, but I had a meeting with him in New York. He picked up the telephone and called me up.

He said, "Could you come to my room?"

I said, "Yeah." I went up to his room.

He said, "I just want you to know that the way I was, I'm not going to be that way anymore."

This [ball] reminds me that it gave me a chance to actually change the minds of some people that wasn't the kind of person they wanted to be. Then, this ball reminds me of the fact that there's more work to be done, to tell the truth. There's more mouths to be fed. There's more work to be done.

Finish this sentence for me: "Baseball is..."

Baseball is a part of life that was born centuries ago that makes you holler "Hallelujah!"

On February 8, 2016, Mudcat received an honorary doctorate of humane letters from Whittier College in California for his dedication to researching and advocating the history of African-Americans in baseball. (Courtesy of Whittier College)

HEROES OF THE SWEET SPOT

JUSTINE
SIEGAL
COACH

JUSTINE SIEGAL

"If you tell a girl she can't play baseball, what else will she think she can't do?"

She is the first woman to pitch batting practice to and coach a Major League Baseball team. When Justine Siegal picks up a baseball, someone is going to learn about throwing a curveball, holding runners on base, or how to play the game the right way. Coaching and mentoring are in her blood, along with a deep love of pitching and the game that's allowed her to put up with the slings and arrows of a society and a culture that sometimes views women as interlopers to the male fraternity that is baseball. This bona fide baseball pioneer is on a mission to make the game fully accessible to girls and women wishing to coach, play, or umpire at any level.

I LOVE THE WAY A BASEBALL feels in my hand when I pitch and either blow a fastball by someone, or that perfect curveball, 3-2 curve. It's the best feeling. I love baseball, and in my family, every meal was, "what are the Indians doing?"

I started with T-ball, and then I ended up playing in Little League. Once we moved to Cleveland, I remember playing ball everywhere. I would ride my bike wherever I could and play sports until I had to come home. I was the only girl, but I was still just part of the gang.

I wanted to be Nolan Ryan and Orel Hershiser. But I didn't have any female role models, as there weren't any to be had.

I started playing baseball and T-ball, and then I kept playing, and I had a really great time, through 12 years old. Then when I was 13, I had a new coach, and he said he didn't want me on his team because "girls play softball." And that was when I decided I would forever play baseball. So I kept playing, and he kept me as shortstop because I was still one of the better players on the team

When I went to high school, they wouldn't let me try out. But then I ended up switching high schools, and they let me try out, and I played against my old high school. I would say that my best moment in baseball was when I got to pitch against the varsity baseball team at the high school that wouldn't let me try out, and I retired the three, four, and five hitters, and the ball never left the infield. I was playing for a guest team, and afterward, the captain of that team asked me if I would go to dinner with the team and hang out with them. I felt included and part of the team, and I got to prove my old team wrong.

Once I graduated, I played college fall ball. In fact, I went to Beloit College because I wanted to play college baseball there. They had a no-cut policy, and I became their first cut, which they said was because they didn't have enough uniforms, which now I know

was a lawsuit. But I didn't know that at the time, so I just kept playing in men's leagues. Then I went to the Colorado Silver Bullets for spring training, and I lost my amateur status.

What are your thoughts about gender discrimination in baseball?

I think it's insane that people want to put a gender to baseball. Baseball's just the greatest game on earth. Why does it matter if you're a boy or a girl or a man or a woman if you want to play? Throwing a curveball is not gender-specific and it's disheartening when people say girls can't play baseball, that it's just for boys.

I see a connection between accessibility of women getting the chance to play baseball, and what's going on in our country and the opportunities that women have in our country. I think all in all, it's about whether we think men and women should have equal opportunities or not. Sometimes, when you look at the news, you don't think everyone thinks that. But I think that baseball has been historically a proving ground for masculinity. It's where men become men.

Whether that ends up being in the business room, whether you're CEO, can a woman do a man's job, can a woman lead a company, or can a woman stand on the mound and take charge? Can a woman lead the field behind home plate as a catcher? You see that reflection between baseball and the real world. But I think you're also seeing a bit of a why-not, as more parents, especially dads, they have daughters, and now they want their daughters to be CEOs.

They want their daughters to be able to have any job that they think they can do. And because of that, they're starting to say, "well, wait a minute, if my daughter wants to play baseball, maybe we should have that opportunity available."

When you play with girls, you show that you respect them. All the girls who play baseball just want to be part of the team. They would like to not even be known as the girl on the team, just a teammate. When boys play with girls, it's saying, "I respect your talents and I respect you as my teammate; let's get the game going."

I worry that if you tell a girl she can't play baseball, what else will she think she can't do? Conversely, if you tell a boy girls don't play baseball, what else will boys think that girls can't do? What kind of America do we want to live in? I think it's really important boys and girls know that anything's possible, that we kind of smash the gender boxes because right now, we've got women who can lead in the military. We have a woman running for president.

We have men who are wonderful nurses, teaching, doing all kinds of jobs that at one point weren't for men, and now we see women doing jobs that at one point weren't for women. So I think we can all pitch.

We're seeing sports such as the NBA and the NFL who have women who are officials on the field now.

I think it's so funny that people think it's a big deal that a woman is an official, as if her sight and hearing are different or as if she can't see the same play. It just doesn't make any sense, because there's not even a physical component to being an official. But it is very exciting to see that more women are getting to show what they can do in a men's professional sport.

Did you play for the US national women's baseball team?

I never played for the national team. I helped start the first national team with USA Baseball, and it was my dream to be able to play for my country, but I didn't think that you could play and lead at the same time. I chose to be in a position where I could build a better future than just thinking about my own career.

I was 16 when I decided I wanted to be a college baseball coach. And the coach I shared that with, he laughed at me and said no man would ever listen to a woman on a baseball field. And that was heartbreaking, but I decided to prove him wrong. Who was he to decide what men would do? And who was he to decide what I could do? From that day forward, I decided I wanted to be a baseball coach and I started training.

I started doing camps, reading, doing anything I could to learn about the game. I did end up becoming a college baseball coach, as an assistant at Springfield College for three years while I got my Ph.D. in sports psychology. The men do listen to you when you know what you're talking about, and you care about them. In 2009, I became the first woman to coach independent or men's professional baseball. I did it in the independent minor leagues with the Brockton Rox.

In 2011, I became the first woman to throw batting practice to a major league team [the Cleveland Indians]. That was like being in the movies, to get to go into the locker room, the Indians were my first team, and there's my jersey hanging with number 15, which is my daughter's number, and just put on the shoes. I always put my socks on first, and then my pants. There's this whole ritual of putting on your uniform.

(Courtesy Cleveland Indians)

My daughter, Jasmine, was there to see the whole thing, and that was incredible. Just this past fall in 2015, I became the first woman to coach for a Major League Baseball organization, and that was with the Oakland Athletics, and it was during fall ball.

Justine with the 2015 Oakland A's Fall Ball
team (Courtesy Justine Siegal)

I asked the A's if I could coach with them, and it took four years for them to say "yes." You don't make the impossible possible by not being extremely persistent. I just kept making my resume better and better in those four years, and I think the timing was right culturally with the NFL and the NBA including more women and it just made sense. I told the A's, "it's going to happen, so let's do it." They said "yes," and I had an amazing time with the A's. It really felt like family.

My time as a guest instructor was for two weeks, instructional weeks, and now, I'm looking for a spot with spring training.

How's that going?

Still looking.

What is Baseball For All?

When I was 23, and I was holding my daughter as a newborn, I decided I didn't want her to struggle to play baseball as I did. I decided I wanted to build opportunities instead of waiting for them. I was young, and I didn't really know what I was doing, but I started a 14-and-under women's league in Cleveland, and then it turned into "how can I help the girls?" And that's when I brought the 12- and-under Sparks to Cooperstown Dreams Park, and we became the first girls' team to compete in a national boys' tournament.

In 2010, after our success with the Sparks in Cooperstown, one of the parents said, "I can help you make this a non-profit." And I said, "yes, for sure," and that is the official birth of Baseball For All, which is a national non-profit for girls who want to get in the game, whether it's playing, umpiring or coaching. Essentially, we empower girls to know that their dreams are worth it.

(Photo by Karl Mondon)

Two baseball legends, Shae Lillywhite and Simone Wearne, are working with Baseball For All.

Through Baseball For All, we have an opportunity for girls to meet players and coaches who are women, which is very important. Shae Lillywhite and Simone Wearne were national team players [for Team Australia], that's a role model. [Wearne is also the first woman to be elected to the Australian Baseball Hall of Fame.]

It's a luxury for these girls to be able to see women who are where they want to be, and that's why it's important and special when we have women like that work with us.

As the chairperson of the Women's Baseball Commission for the World Baseball Softball Confederation, part of my responsibility is to see girls and women's baseball grow internationally. So I have seen Simone and Lilly grow up through the system, and I was very excited when Simone was named the manager of the Australian national [women's] team last year. It's great to see those kinds of strides.

What is Perry Barber's relationship to Baseball For All?

Perry Barber is an umpire extraordinaire, and a huge role model for our girls. She's helped us emphasize umpiring as an option, as

Perry Barber, Umpire

a path for girls, whether they're working in high school or they want to go professionally.

Something we did that was really special last year at our nationals tournament was, we had all of our girls go through umpiring stations, so that they could learn the beginnings, and then half our umpires in the tournament were women.

So not only did the girls get to experience what umpiring is like, but they got to see role models like Perry actually in their game. I know that Perry is sort of leading that movement of umpires, so I'm really proud of her.

Maybelle Blair and Shirley Burkovich, former players from the All-American Girls Professional Baseball League, are involved with your program. What has that meant to Baseball For All?

Maybelle Blair, pitcher

Shirley Burkovich, utility, Springfield Sallies

It means a lot for Baseball For All to be able to unite with women from the All-American Girls Professional Baseball League. Our players love meeting Maybelle and Shirley. Not only are they hilarious and have great stories of when they were playing, but there's a spirit of inspiration that comes out when you meet them, and they were trailblazers for our girls.

Ozzie Sailors, former pitcher for Team USA, is also involved. What's her role in this movement?

Ozzie Sailors is almost the heart of this movement. I've never met a player, a female player with more passion than Ozzie. She just breathes this game. She's a real inspiration for our girls because she, too, was told by a very prominent pitching coach that she should quit, when she was in high school, and play lacrosse. Now, she's not just pitching at the college level but she's the captain of her team [the men's baseball team at University of Presque Isle, Maine].

Her hat is in the National Baseball Hall of Fame and here she is, inspiring all our girls. And she's just another example; if you listen to those naysayers, nothing ever gets done.

I had many challenges trying to play baseball as a female, not just the easy ones which were getting the opportunity to try out. People were mean. One of my good friends said it was against God's way for me to play baseball. But I'm one of the lucky ones, because I know too many women who have tried to play a male sport and they've been physically attacked.

It's pretty sad that I consider myself the lucky one when I probably have enough trauma from just trying to play the game. I think it's the matter of the way people talk to you or even the way people don't talk to you, and the stares, and the things that people shout at you, the swear words, the sexual words, while you're trying to play the game, while you're trying to pitch. One of my players was hit every single time she was at bat, just trying to play high school baseball. The entire league decided they would hit her. I just don't understand it. Of course, until actually, I understood it, it's a threat to the idea of what's masculine, in some imaginary world of what is masculine. But it's not easy to play this game if you're a female with a passion for it. You have to have very thick skin.

I started the baseball organization for my daughter so that she would have the opportunities to play and Jasmine has no interest in playing baseball. Which is okay with me, because really, if you think about Baseball For All, it's all about being who you want to be, and not letting a gender box tame you. And my daughter is not tamed by anybody. The one thing my daughter knows from watching me is that anything's possible, and she's taking that on her own path.

Have you experienced any surprises in the process of leading Baseball For All?

These girls, when you see them, and they meet you, and when they're playing with other girls, the smiles on their faces, it's just priceless. And when a girl writes a school report on you, it's humbling, and that's why I do it. It's an honor to make history, but it's much more important we build a better future.

(Photo by Karl Mondon)

In ten years, I see Baseball For All as the continued leader of girls' baseball, continuing to advocate and continuing to educate. I think the goal is that Baseball For All inspires girls' baseball leagues all around the country.

I've thought about my goals and achievements. Do you know what? I'm 40, and I've achieved most of my goals. My daughter said I have to build new ones. I think I'd like to get to spring training with a major league team, and I'd like to do more work with Major League Baseball to continue to grow the game, and make sure that it is a game available to everyone. I'd just like to see girls playing baseball around the country. That's my goal.

Is there a coaching position you're interested in at the major league level?

It would be more natural for me to be a pitching coach since I was a pitcher. I've been working more and more on understanding the game at a further level. I think that my strength is that players generally like me, and they feel safe with me, and I can use my Ph.D. in sports psychology to sort of communicate what the hitting coach is trying to say and what the player is trying to say, and make it all work.

I think the trust with the players is something I bring to a pitching staff, and I think diversity is important and not all coaches bring trust. They bring orders.

Every coach and every person has their own communication style, but as a woman who knows the game, who's played the game, who's coached the game, who has a Ph.D. in sports psychology, even just having been a mother, you bring all that to the table.

I think I'm a huge asset to a team because when you create diversity in your staff, all of a sudden, you create a formula to be inclusive, to get the players to feel like they're trusted and that they can go somewhere.

If everyone has the same talents and everyone's bringing the same thing, then you just end up with a coaching staff that's stale. I think I can be a little firecracker, maybe a quiet firecracker but one that makes a difference.

If you could leave a message to baseball fans 200 years from now, what would it be?

I think 200 years from now, people are going to laugh and be shocked by how mistreated girls and women were in this game. But my message to them would be, "See? Isn't baseball a game for all, after all?"

ACKNOWLEDGEMENTS

After thirty years in the entertainment industry, we've learned one core principle: you need a strong team of people working with you to achieve goals. And so it goes for *Baseball Pioneers*.

Many thanks to our interviewees, who were brave enough to sit for interviews lasting anywhere from twenty minutes to two hours (as well as providing images from their collections): Perry Barber, Maybelle Blair, Shirley Burkovich, Jim "Mudcat" Grant, and Ron Rapoport. Trudy Grant, Mudcat's wife, gets an assist for opening their home to us.

Photographs were of critical importance to this book. We are most grateful to John Horne of the National Baseball Hall of Fame photo archive, along with Jeremy Feador and the Cleveland Indians, the Minnesota Twins, and the Pittsburgh Pirates. Bob Cullum and the Boston Public Library provided exquisite images of the Boston Red Sox from the Leslie Jones Collection. The Center for History in Indiana has one of the most extensive photographic collections of the All-American Girls Professional Baseball League and were most helpful. We also appreciate the assistance of the Negro Leagues Museum, the Institute for Baseball Studies, and Whittier College.

We thank our friends from the Society for American Baseball

Research (SABR) for image support, too: Jacob Pomrenke, Stephanie Liscio, and Joseph Wancho.

Graphic artist Brian Kruse has become a trusted creative partner on *The Sweet Spot* team, and we are thrilled with his cover art.

Donna Eden Cohen is a long-time friend who has provided invaluable support to us working with Maybelle Blair and Shirley Burkovich, Justine Siegal, Ozzie Sailors, and Perry Barber.

The legendary Arnold Hano was kind enough to write the foreword for this book, and we are indeed honored to have his words grace this project.

Lastly, we thank you, dear reader, for making our first book part of your treasured collection

— *Kelly Holtzclaw and Jon Leonoudakis*
Los Angeles, Winter, 2018

Made in the USA
San Bernardino, CA
13 March 2018